A SEASON FOR THE AGES

A SEASON FOR THE AGES

How the 2016 Chicago Cubs Brought a
World Series Championship to the North Side

Al Yellon

Foreword by Pat Hughes

SPORTS
PUBLISHING

Sports Publishing books may be purchased in bulk at special discounts for sales promotion, corporate gifts, fund-raising, or educational purposes. Special editions can also be created to specifications. For details, contact the Special Sales Department, Sports Publishing, 307 West 36th Street, 11th Floor, New York, NY 10018 or sportspubbooks@skyhorsepublishing.com.

Sports Publishing® is a registered trademark of Skyhorse Publishing, Inc.®, a Delaware corporation.

Visit our website at www.sportspubbooks.com.

10 9 8 7 6 5 4 3 2

Library of Congress Cataloging-in-Publication Data is available on file.

Cover design by Tom Lau and Brian Peterson
Cover photo credit: Associated Press

ISBN 978-1-68358-115-4
Ebook ISBN: 978-1-68358-116-1

Printed in the United States of America

CONTENTS

This is for everyone who has ever loved the Cubs but did not make it to this day.
We, the living, carry your torch and celebrate for you and with you in spirit.
Go Cubs!

Foreword

The Chicago Cubs came into the 2016 season with very high hopes. Not only was that fueled by the 2015 postseason run, but during the 2015–16 offseason the Cubs front office made great strides toward fortifying the ballclub, signing Ben Zobrist, John Lackey, and Jason Heyward, all three of whom played roles in the success of this 2016 team. They surely would have been a solid contender even without those three guys, and the emergence of young players such as Javier Baez, Willson Contreras, Carl Edwards Jr., and the real blossoming of Addison Russell at shortstop are among the reasons this team was so dominant early in the season.

Al Yellon's book takes you on the ride from spring training through the end of the World Series, detailing this glorious year, and here are some of my favorite moments from the 2016 season.

First, the amazing start of 25–6—that's winning 80 percent of your games! Starting that way gives you even higher hopes. They were winning the Series on the road: sweeping the Pirates at PNC Park, and winning at home: sweeping the Nationals at Wrigley Field, culminated with Javier Baez' extra-inning walk-off home run.

You do those things and you start thinking: "This really is a special team!"

The struggles the Cubs had in late June and early July are just part of the game, part of the daily grind. Pitchers aren't going to have their best stuff every day and they're going to struggle at times. But I knew this team was too good to play that way for too long. And they beat the Pirates at PNC Park to right the ship just before the All-Star break.

Right after that break is when the Cubs really begin to hit their stride with great pitching, great fielding, and clutch hitting—Anthony Rizzo had a big three-run double against Will Smith in Milwaukee in late July.

If there was a signature game that represented a major turning point from where the Cubs were a very good team to potentially a great team, it came on a magical Sunday night, July 31 at Wrigley against Seattle. The Cubs fell behind 6–0 early. They were still down by three runs in the bottom of the ninth when they rallied to tie the game and in extra innings, Jon Lester laid down a safety squeeze bunt driving in Jason Heyward with the winning run. For me, that would be the most exciting moment in a season full of exciting moments. After the game, Joe Maddon said that's the kind of a win where you can really propel your team to greater heights.

Joe wasn't kidding—that win began an 11-game winning streak for the Cubs. They were never seriously threatened by anybody in the division thereafter. They waltzed to the division title, clinching with more than two weeks to go, eliminating the Cardinals from the race. And everyone knew the Cubs were going to be ready for the postseason.

They beat the Giants in a classic in the opener: Javier Baez's solo home run in the eighth inning settled a pitcher's duel between Jon Lester and Johnny Cueto, and then there was the miraculous four-run rally in the ninth inning in Game 4 in San Francisco that gave the ballclub the Division Series victory.

Then it was onto take on the Dodgers and you knew that would be tough as they have the best pitcher on the planet, Clayton Kershaw, who beat the Cubs in Game 2 to even the series.

After a Game 3 loss at Dodger Stadium, the Cubs came roaring back on home runs by Addison Russell in Games 4 and 5 and then in Game 6, an absolute masterpiece by Kyle Hendricks. The young right-hander outpitched Kershaw and the Cubs offense provided plenty of support.

It was one of the greatest moments in Cubs history when Yasiel Puig bounced to short which turned into a 6–4–3 game-ending and series-clinching double play, one of the most exciting moments I've ever experienced.

When Puig hit into that double play, it was the thrill of a lifetime for me as the Cubs broadcaster to be able to finally say: "The Cubs are going to the World Series! The Cubs win the pennant!" Those were words I'd been aching to say for 21 seasons, and I thought about all of the great Cubs, particularly Mr. Cub, Ernie Banks, and my dear friend Ron Santo, who would have loved to have been there. I was thrilled with the fact that Billy Williams and Fergie Jenkins were there along with Kerry Wood, Bobby Dernier, and Gary Matthews. I thought of others like Randy Hundley, Glenn Beckert, Don Kessinger, Kenny Holtzman, and all the Cubs of yesteryear. I was thrilled that those men were still very much alive and could experience that.

And I thought about the Cubs' longtime TV broadcasters Harry Caray and Jack Brickhouse. And before me in the radio booth, people like Vince Lloyd, Lou Boudreau, Jack Quinlan, all of whom would have loved to be there for that moment. It was a very emotional time and it was extremely exciting—the Cubs winning the pennant for the first time since 1945 and then it was on to the World Series.

The Cubs felt very good about themselves after winning the pennant. Onto Game 1 in Cleveland, where the Cubs faced Corey Kluber who proved to be mysterious and difficult to hit. The Cubs got shut out and surprisingly, Indians catcher Roberto Perez, of all people, hit two home runs.

The next night, however, the Cubs' offense awoke and they were able to beat the Tribe in Cleveland to even up the Series at one victory apiece.

The Cubs knew then they could come home to Wrigley Field with a chance to possibly win the World Series without having to go back to the airport. However, that feeling quickly was dismissed because they lost the first home World Series game at Wrigley since 1945, 1–0.

The next day, the Cubs felt a disaster was possibly right around the corner as they lost, 7–2, and now, all of a sudden, the Cubs are on the brink of elimination after this magical season where they had won 103 games.

Only five teams had ever come back from trailing three games to one to win the World Series and only three had done it by winning Games 6 and 7 on the road, which the Cubs would've had to do.

Game 5 represented a turnaround. National League MVP candidate Kris Bryant homered as part of a three-run inning and the Cubs would not trail for the remainder of the series. Jon Lester pitched great ball and Aroldis Chapman closed out the game as the Cubs stayed alive with a 3–2 win.

And so it was back to Cleveland. Game 6 was a blowout, with Bryant hitting another home run and Addison Russell having one of the biggest games ever in the World Series, smashing the first grand slam in Cubs World Series history and driving in six, and all of a sudden it was down to Game 7.

And what an amazing game it was. I knew, being a Cub broadcaster and a Cub fan, that Game 7 would not be easy—easy was just not meant to be in this World Series!

The Cubs began well, with Dexter Fowler leading off the game with a home run. Eight different players for the Cubs drove in runs in one of the wildest games you will ever see. David Ross, playing in his final big league game, belted a home run against ace reliever Andrew Miller. Javy Baez also hit a home run and the Cubs looked like they were going to win the game in regulation, leading 6–3 in the eighth only to have the Indians come storming back with a home run by Rajai Davis off Aroldis Chapman to tie the game at 6.

The Indians would not score, neither would the Cubs in the ninth inning, and so it was on to the 10th.

Kyle Schwarber, who made that remarkable recovery from the knee surgery in April, led off the pivotal 10th with a single into right field. Albert Almora went in to pinch run and on a fly ball by Kris Bryant, Almora alertly tagged up and went to second. Anthony Rizzo was walked intentionally, and then Ben Zobrist, who would become the World Series MVP, doubled sharply down the left-field line, scoring Almora with the go-ahead run. A single by Miguel Montero would give the Cubs an insurance run that turned out to actually be the winning margin because the Indians, with two out in the bottom of the 10th inning, scored a run.

Then Mike Montgomery, the tall long-legged lefthander, came in to get the final out, Michael Martinez grounding to Kris Bryant who fired to Rizzo—fittingly, the two superstars on the team ending up on the final play—and the Cubs won the game, 8–7, and the World Series.

For me as a broadcaster, it was a dramatic moment. I said, "The Chicago Cubs win the World Series and the longest drought in the history of American sports is over and the celebration begins!"

It was a great thrill, the thrill of my lifetime to be the Cubs' voice at that moment. I thought about all the great fans and the multi-generations of fans that have followed this team and finally, finally! The Cubs are the World Series champions. Life is good.

Those are some of my thoughts on this most magnificent of Cubs seasons. This book is filled with more details, as well as tracing the journey of both the team, Al as a Cubs fan, and as to how we got to this time of triumph. And away we go . . .

—Pat Hughes
Broadcaster, Chicago Cubs
670 The Score

Introduction

A World Series on Chicago's North Side

Most of all, this is a love story.

All of us fell in love with the Chicago Cubs at some point in our lives, whether it was because of a childhood trip to Wrigley Field, team fandom passed down from grandparent to parent to child, or being exposed to the team through WGN-TV, even if you never lived in Chicago.

And for years, decades, it was unrequited love. Year after year after year, the Cubs never made it this far. Sometimes, the season was over by the end of April, yet we persevered, watching 90-plus loss teams drag through dull Septembers. Other times, our love was crushed in jaw-dropping fashion, so close to the ultimate goal.

Yet we continued. The love was too deep to be ruined, even by loss after loss after loss. "Maybe next year" was a mantra stated by fan to fan every October as we watched other teams play in the World Series, wondering if our time would ever come.

And then, almost suddenly, it was here, November 2, 2016, a date which will be remembered forever by Cubs fans, baseball fans, even people who don't care about sports but who got pulled into this story—a story of resilience and comeback and heroic performances under the most pressure imaginable in a sports contest. At last, the Cubs returned our love, in the most magnificent way we could have imagined.

The Cubs are World Series champions.

I keep saying that and thinking it and now I've written it and read it and it still seems somewhat unbelievable. No living person had been able to say that or write it or read it until now—sure, there are a few people living today born before October 14, 1908, but I'd bet that none of them were Chicago Cubs or even baseball fans on that day when the Cubs won the World Series in Detroit.

Now there are thousands who can say they were actually there, and millions more who are thrilled, by the Cubs' win over the Cleveland Indians in the World Series.

Writing these words about how it happened still seems somewhat surreal. It's been such a dream, a quest, for Cubs fans for so many years and decades that now that it's become reality, it might take quite some time for everyone to process what we've just seen.

As preparations for the Cubs' first World Series in 71 years began, the biggest surprise for everyone was the last-minute addition of Kyle Schwarber to the World Series roster. Schwarber, who was ruled out for the season after his horrifying knee injury on April 7, had been ruled out for the playoffs again by Theo Epstein as recently as the end of August.

But Schwarber had worked very, very hard in his rehab and had been seen working out on the field at Wrigley at times during the summer, even running a bit wearing a knee brace.

When he was cleared to hit by his doctors, he made a plea to Theo to at least give him a chance. The team sent him to hit off a pitching machine. Schwarber later said he saw 1,300 pitches from the machine, seemingly set to "11" (on the "Spinal Tap" scale) so he could hit the toughest possible pitches. Then they sent him to play two games in the Arizona Fall League, where he went 1-for-6 with two walks and was pronounced ready to DH for the Cubs in the games played in Cleveland.

Bud Selig's nonsensical "This Time It Counts" prevented Miriam and me from seeing the first Cubs World Series game in our lifetimes in person. The Cubs should have had home-field advantage because they won 103 games to the Indians' 94.

But they didn't, and Game 1 was in Cleveland Tuesday, October 25. I'd have loved to have been there. But several factors intervened. First was the cost. I'd been lucky enough to score face-value tickets for the games in San Francisco and Los Angeles for the previous rounds, and of course I had tickets to all the games at Wrigley Field as a full-season ticket holder.

But I came up empty trying to get face-value tickets in Cleveland. (I had them for Blue Jays games in Toronto—for that reason I had wished the Jays had won the AL pennant instead.) And the prices in Cleveland on the secondary market were too high for me, and beyond that, having arrived back from Los Angeles at midnight the day before Game 6 of the NLCS and then staying up way too late to celebrate the Game 6 win, I didn't trust myself to drive the six hours to Cleveland safely.

So, instead, for the first time in the postseason, I watched a Cubs game on TV, after I had headed to a memorabilia store tucked in an out-of-the-way neighborhood on the northwest side of Chicago to buy some Cubs World Series garb. This was easier than fighting the crowds in Wrigleyville, plus free parking! I bought a couple of World Series caps and a National League Champions T-shirt, but wanted to save my money for . . . World Series Champions merchandise.

Unlike many, I don't mind Joe Buck as an announcer. He calls a competent game and since Fox replaced Tim McCarver with John Smoltz as an analyst, I think Buck has become better at his craft. He and Smoltz make a good team.

Game 1, unfortunately, wasn't much worth watching. Jon Lester, who entered the game with an 0.43 World Series ERA in three previous starts, loaded the bases in the first inning on a single and two walks. Another single scored a run and then Lester hit Brandon Guyer with a pitch to force in another run.

This is Guyer's game—he sets up in order to try to get hit. It's an art, actually, because by rule umpires are not supposed to allow you to take a base if they think you are not trying to get out of the way. Somehow Guyer does—he led the major leagues in HBP in 2016 despite having only 345 plate appearances.

In a 2–0 hole with Corey Kluber on the mound and Andrew Miller lurking in the pen, the Cubs really had no chance. A Roberto Perez homer made it 3–0 Cleveland going into the seventh, but then it was Miller time. (Sorry, had to use that line once here. That'll be the only time you'll see it.)

The Cubs actually got to Miller, sort of. Two singles (one by Schwarber, who had doubled and barely missed a homer earlier) and a walk loaded the bases with no one out in the seventh, but Willson Contreras flied to center, too short to score a run, and Addison Russell and David Ross struck out. In the eighth, Kris Bryant walked and Ben Zobrist singled, bringing up Schwarber with two out.

This series hadn't gotten to fairy-tale country yet. Miller struck out Schwarber to end the inning.

The Cubs might still have had a chance in the ninth; Miller had to leave the game after throwing 46 pitches, the most he had thrown since becoming a full-time reliever in 2012. But after a two-out walk and single off Justin Grimm, Hector Rondon entered. Instead of putting out the fire, he served up a three-run homer to Perez, his second of the game—this from someone who hit .183 with three home runs all year—and the Cubs went down to a dull 6–0 defeat.

So it was up to Jake Arrieta to be the Jake! of the second half of 2015 in Game 2, because the Cubs certainly would not want to go down two games to one.

And he was. Jake flirted with history, throwing 5⅓ no-hit innings before Jason Kipnis doubled in the sixth. By then the Cubs had a 5–0 lead. They scored quickly off Trevor Bauer in the first inning on a single by Kris Bryant and double by Anthony Rizzo, plated another in the third when Rizzo walked, Ben Zobrist singled and Schwarber drove Rizzo in.

Three Cubs runs followed in the fifth inning. Zobrist tripled and scored on a single by Schwarber, who then advanced to second on a wild pitch—no apparent issues with running the bases for Kyle!

Willson Contreras reached on an error, advancing Schwarber to third, and Jorge Soler walked. Addison Russell then walked, forcing in the third Cubs run of the inning.

The only sour note in the Cubs' 5–1 win was the run the Indians scored, ruining the shutout. After Kipnis's double, he advanced to third on an infield out and scored on a wild pitch. But Mike Montgomery and Aroldis Chapman shut down the Tribe the rest of the way and the series headed to Wrigley Field tied at one game each.

Before Game 3, there was another "Schwarber Watch," as both fans and the team thought, after his outstanding hitting performance in Games 1 and 2, that perhaps he could play the outfield in the Wrigley games, to keep his bat in the lineup.

Everyone—fans, media, assorted hangers-on—waited for the team's pregame news conference on the Series off-day, Thursday, October 27, for word from team doctors.

Theo Epstein didn't waste any time putting forth the news to reporters. While Kyle's doctors had cleared him to hit and run the bases, they felt that the unexpected cuts and turns that an outfielder might have to make would be too risky for Kyle to play the field. They said he'd only be "about 60 percent," and Kyle simply wasn't wired to play that way. It was the safe, prudent thing to do, though it would limit Schwarber to only pinch-hitting at Wrigley. He did, though, get the loudest ovation of any Cubs player during the Game 3 player introductions.

Miriam and I left for Wrigley Field earlier than usual for Game 3, to avoid anticipated congestion in the neighborhood.

Wow, did we underestimate things. There were hundreds of people walking up and down Sheffield and Waveland Avenues near the bleachers. I'd say 95 percent of them didn't have tickets; they were just there either to get into the bars to watch the games, or just to soak up the atmosphere. Some of them lined up near the ticket windows on Clark Street, hoping to get a ticket to the game. Of those, some had been there for nearly 24 hours when a small handful of tickets were actually released at face value, rewarding them for their wait.

Police presence was robust, but friendly. Most of the Chicago police officers wore neon-yellow vests for visibility and were smiling, happy to answer questions from either neighborhood regulars or those who were first-timers to Wrigleyville.

By 3:30 or so the area was crowded enough that police began to shut down streets, first Sheffield and Waveland, then the area around Clark and Addison. Season-ticket holders had been sent emails to expect the gates to open at 4:30, 30 minutes earlier than you'd expect for a 7 p.m. game. But even that wound up being changed, as the Cubs got their gameday staff in place a bit early so the gates could open and relieve crowd pressure on the streets.

And then, it was World Series time at Wrigley Field.

In some ways, it was just like a regular-season game. There were the sounds of bat against ball for batting practice, recorded music and Gary Pressy's organ playing familiar tunes.

But there were also signs that this was no ordinary game. TV cameras everywhere. Extra platforms for still cameras taking up almost every inch of extra concourse space behind us in the left-field bleachers. About half the 500-level seats on the left-field side taken up for an auxiliary media area, as was part of the usual ADA seating area in the upper deck beneath the press box. World Series trivia and history on the video boards.

The World Series—at Wrigley Field! Something no one had seen in 71 years. Stories abounded of older men and women who had been at World Series games in 1945, attending again, thrilled that they lived to see this day. Stories of kids like Frank Colletti, 11 years old in 1945, deemed "too young" to go to the World Series with his dad and brothers, but promised he could go to "the next one." Well... of course, there was no "next one" until now, but 82-year-old Frank Colletti was taken to the World Series by his nephew Ned—a former Cubs front office executive, later general manager of the Dodgers.

It's things like those that bind generations of Cubs fans together, the game handed down from grandfather to father to son (and, not to leave anyone out, grandmother to mother to daughter), the 102-year-old ballpark different now with lights and video boards, but in essence still the same ballyard where families have shared baseball all these years.

Hall of Famer Billy Williams threw out a ceremonial first pitch for Game 3, and while that was an honor for Billy, it also brought back a bit of sadness, knowing that Ernie Banks would likely have had that distinction if he'd still been living, as would Ron Santo for one of the World Series games. Every Cubs fan, I believe, wished Ernie and Ron could have been there for the day we'd all been waiting for all our lives.

If only all those Hall of Famers could have helped the Cubs' bats that night. Kyle Hendricks didn't give up a run—but he also didn't make it out of the fifth inning, constantly in trouble with hits (six of them) and, uncharacteristically, walks. The wind was blowing out strongly during Game 3 and that could have been a bit of Hendricks's issue, as he needs pinpoint command to succeed.

The wind might have also psyched out Cubs hitters. This is something they commonly tell each other not to do, but they couldn't get anything going offensively, with just two hits through six innings. In the seventh, Carl Edwards Jr. allowed a leadoff single to Roberto Perez. Pinch-runner Michael Martinez advanced to second on a sacrifice and was wild-pitched to third. Following a walk, Edwards gave up an RBI single to Coco Crisp.

Still, 1–0 and with Andrew Miller long out of the game, perhaps the Cubs could still come back. Before that, though, fans were treated to Bill Murray's odd "Daffy Duck" rendition of "Take Me Out to the Ball Game." (Daffy Duck? Cubs baseball? Do those go together in your mind? Me, neither.)

Jorge Soler tripled with two out in the seventh, but was stranded. Meanwhile, Mike Montgomery, Pedro Strop, and Aroldis Chapman held the Indians scoreless through the top of the ninth.

In the bottom of the inning, Anthony Rizzo singled. With the situation desperate, Joe Maddon sent Chris Coghlan in to run for Rizzo, even though that would mean a defensive downgrade if the game went into extras.

Zobrist struck out. Willson Contreras grounded out, with Coghlan taking second. Then Jason Heyward hit a ground ball right to Mike Napoli at first. The crowd, as one, groaned. Game over, right?

No! Napoli booted it, and Heyward was safe with Coghlan taking third. The tying run, now just 90 feet away!

Heyward stole second while Javier Baez was batting. This meant that if Baez could only bounce a single into center field, just as he had done in Game 4 in San Francisco, the Cubs would win the game.

You know the saying, right? "If wishes were horses . . ."

Baez ran the count to 2–2 and then swung and missed on a pitch that was near his eyes. Javy's an exciting player, many times rising to the occasion and his defense is beyond impeccable. But there are times he tries to hit a 900-foot home run with every swing. This wasn't the time for that, and as a result, the Cubs went down two games to one.

The neighborhood, if anything, was even more crowded with people as we arrived about noon for Game 4—yes, even seven hours to game time. Many of these people had, again, arrived without tickets nor any idea where they'd watch the game. Some bars in the area were trying to take advantage of the situation by charging huge cover fees just to get in, this in an area where covers had never, ever been charged before. Reports of anywhere from $100 to $250 for certain Wrigleyville bars—and I won't shame them by naming them here—circulated around the area. Even with these charges, some places wound up overcrowded and were cited by police and shut down for exceeding occupancy limits.

Again, CPD did an excellent job securing the perimeter of the ballpark so as to try to keep the numbers of people in the immediate surrounding area down. Even so, the crowds were huge. I wound up running into Michelle, an old friend who used to work security at the ballpark but who now works as an EMT in Philadelphia, who stopped by to say hello, as well as other friends who did wind up spending the big money just so they could say they saw a World Series game at Wrigley Field.

Attempts to get from my seat in the bleachers to the other side of the park to say hello to friends sitting there wound up taking several times as long as usual, as all the aisles and concourses were swarmed quite early. I did, at last, find a way back to the bleachers that was relatively untraveled, but I think I'll keep that to myself, a mental note for the next World Series at Wrigley.

If people spent $1,700 (the reported lowest price for standing room) or $2,400 (among the lowest prices for an actual seat) for Saturday's game, I hope they felt it was worth being in the atmosphere.

Because the game certainly wasn't worth it, perhaps the worst performance of all by the Cubs in the postseason. Game 4 wasn't going to be easy, not with Corey Kluber throwing again for the second time in four days, but John Lackey had made lots of brave talk about pitching well in "big-boy games," as he called them.

Lackey sure didn't pitch, nor act, like a "big boy" in this one. He often lets himself get upset over ball-and-strike calls and this act isn't going to help him get those calls. He was also victimized by a couple of Kris Bryant errors in the second inning, including one on a weakly hit ball by Kluber, who was batting with the bases loaded after an intentional walk with the score still tied 1–1. The Cubs had scored first on a double by Dexter Fowler and single by Anthony Rizzo, but they coughed it right back in that second inning, when Kluber rolled a slow grounder down the third-base line. Bryant, who had already made a wild throw earlier in the inning after a slick pickup, probably should have eaten the ball, and pulled Rizzo off first base with his throw, allowing a run to score.

The Indians extended the lead to 3–1 in the third, and the Cubs couldn't do anything with Kluber. Lackey lasted five innings, his longest outing of the postseason, and his defense didn't do him any favors. It might be that age—he turned 38 during the postseason—was finally catching up to Lackey.

The game was 4–1 in the top of the seventh, perhaps still within reach even with Andrew Miller still in the game, but after a Coco Crisp double off Justin Grimm, Grimm hit Rajai Davis with a pitch. That brought Joe out to replace Grimm with Travis Wood to face the left-handed-hitting Jason Kipnis.

Wood ran the count to 3–1 and then Kipnis deposited a ball in the bleachers he'd always admired as a kid growing up in north suburban Northbrook.

It was 7–1. Fans stuck around for Vince Vaughn to sing the seventh-inning stretch, but after the Cubs went down 1-2-3 in the bottom of the inning, a few began to trickle out. Not like they would at Dodger Stadium, but still, small pockets of empty seats appeared. I suppose I couldn't blame them much, late on Saturday evening with the Cubs seemingly hopelessly behind . . . still, I'd never leave a World Series game early.

Those who left missed Dexter Fowler's leadoff homer in the eighth off Miller. That was significant for a couple of reasons: it was another "since 1945" moment, the first Cubs homer in a World Series game since Phil Cavarretta in Game 1 in 1945, and the first for a Cub in the Series at Wrigley Field since Chuck Klein in Game 6 in 1935.

Think about that for a moment. Before Fowler, the last time a Cub homered in the World Series at Wrigley, the current brick-and-ivy configuration of the bleachers was two years away from existing.

That was also the first run scored off Miller in the postseason—ever. He'd thrown 24 previous postseason innings without allowing a single run. So there's that, at least.

But that was it, and the large crowd filed out of Wrigley Field mostly silent, knowing Sunday's Game 5 would be do-or-die.

Sunday in Wrigleyville dawned much quieter than Saturday. Perhaps it was being down three games to one, perhaps it was just that it was Sunday and people get going more slowly on Sundays

than Saturdays, perhaps it was the fall chill finally in the air—
after two very pleasant days for baseball Friday and Saturday with
temperatures in the 60s, it barely cracked 50 all day Sunday with
winds blowing off Lake Michigan, a day that felt more like April at
Wrigley Field. In general, though, the Cubs really lucked out with
weather for all three home dates, considering the calendar almost
showed November. It wasn't brutally cold and there was no rain
interrupting the proceedings.

Crowds did finally show up, but much later than they had for
the two previous games. Even so, the Cubs got folks in place and
opened the ballpark at 4:15 to allow for easier entry and to avoid
bottlenecks. It worked; I heard no issues with people getting into
the park, and just one somewhat horrifying incident. One man had
his ticket swiped right out of his hand just before entering the park
by a woman who started running down the street. Fortunately,
security saw this happen and quickly stopped her and got the
man's ticket back.

Sunday was going to be a bittersweet day at the ballpark regardless of the result, because we knew that it was the final day of baseball at Wrigley Field in this most wonderful of seasons. Still, the
Cubs had gotten to the World Series and extended the baseball
season by a month in Chicago, to the latest calendar day the franchise had ever played. I had hoped to see orange, red or yellow ivy
on the walls at Wrigley Field, but hardly any leaves had changed
color by this late-October Sunday, just a few leaves having turned
a dull shade of brown.

Some fans had been a bit put off by MLB's choice of Patrick Stump from the rock band Fall Out Boy to sing the national
anthem for Game 3, this, even though Stump's a Chicago-area
native and Cubs fan. So it was much better for Game 4 when John
Vincent, a Wrigley regular, did the anthem and Ben Zobrist's wife
Julianna, a professional pop singer, did a soaringly beautiful "God
Bless America." But for feeling at home, there was nothing like
hearing Wayne Messmer, who has been a Wrigley regular singer
for more than 20 years (and former Cubs PA announcer), do both

those songs for Game 5—just as he does for most Sundays during the regular season.

It felt like home.

And so did the game, which might have been the best baseball game I have ever seen, given what was at stake—potential elimination for the Cubs, possible jubilation for the Tribe, something no Cubs fan wanted to see especially after having to witness the Mets celebrating the NL title on our field in 2015.

This time, Lester was on his game, at least at first. He struck out the side in the first inning, then made one mistake with two out in the second, serving up a home-run ball to Jose Ramirez. It could have been worse, but David Ross and Anthony Rizzo teamed up on a catch of a foul popup reminiscent of the one that Pete Rose and Bob Boone pulled off in the World Series in 1980.

The Cubs went down meekly in the second and third against Trevor Bauer, but Kris Bryant brought the crowd to its feet with a home run barely into the first row in left-center field. Bryant had not been hitting well up to then in the Series (1-for-14) so that homer was a welcome sight not just for tying up the game, but putting Bryant back on the right track. The crowd got even louder as hits by Rizzo, Ben Zobrist, and Addison Russell made it 3–1 Cubs.

During this game I downloaded a sound-meter app for my phone. At times during Game 5 it registered 92 decibels—which is an unbelievable level for an outdoor ballpark that's not enclosed.

The Indians pushed across a second run off Lester in the sixth, and Carl Edwards Jr. relieved him in the seventh. C.J. gave up a single to Mike Napoli and a passed ball advanced him to second.

That's when Joe Maddon decided to roll the dice in an elimination game and call on Aroldis Chapman with eight outs to go and a runner on base, something Maddon wouldn't do in a regular-season game and something Chapman isn't used to.

But this is the World Series, and a win was needed. Chapman struck out the first man he faced, barely touching 100 miles per hour. He hit Brandon Guyer—who hasn't?—but then got Roberto

Perez to end the inning on a routine groundout that seemingly was handled with more care than usual by Javier Baez.

I'm not generally a big fan of most of the Cubs' seventh-inning stretch singers. Many of them have only tenuous connections to the Cubs, baseball or Chicago, and some are just there to promote a movie or TV show.

But Eddie Vedder, internationally known singer, is also a Cubs fan. A genuine Cubs fan, not a celebrity hanger-on, a true, live-and-die-with-the-team fan.

And his stretch rendition, seamlessly mixed with video of Harry Caray on the video boards while simultaneously giving love to the retiring David Ross, was perfect for the night, for the occasion, for every Cubs fan in the ballpark and watching around the world on TV. Thank you, Eddie. You knew exactly how every single one of us felt that final Wrigley night of 2016.

Chapman continued. He allowed a one-out hit to Rajai Davis in the eighth, mainly because he didn't get off the mound fast enough to cover first base. Davis stole second and third, but Chapman slipped a 101 mile-per-hour fastball past Francisco Lindor for strike three to end the inning. (Truth be told . . . that pitch was borderline. We'll take it.)

Jason Heyward singled with one out in the bottom of the eighth and stole second. When Baez also struck out, that brought the pitcher's spot to the plate. No one was warming up; everyone in the park knew Maddon was going to stick with Chapman, so he'd have to bat.

Which he had done exactly twice in his major-league career. He walked up to the same Rage Against the Machine song he'd entered the game to an inning before.

He stood in the left-hand batter's box waggling his bat as if he did this sort of thing every day. Give Chapman credit, he put together a pretty good at-bat, during which Heyward stole third. This seemingly odd play had thought behind it, apparently—Heyward's likely trying to draw a bad throw that would allow him to score, since it was unlikely Chapman would get a hit to drive him in, and if Heyward were thrown out, Chapman wasn't going to bat if the game got to the last of the ninth.

Which Chapman made sure didn't happen. Coming in for the ninth, the Wrigley DJ played Chapman's entry song and video again—perhaps just to make him feel like this was familiar territory, coming into the game in the ninth inning, a "clean" inning, no one on base and a one-run lead.

Napoli grounded to short. One out!

Carlos Santana lifted a fly ball near the right-field bullpen, caught by Heyward. Two out!

Wrigley Field itself seemed to stand in anticipation. MLB Network's postgame crew of Greg Amsinger, Harold Reynolds, Al Leiter, and Mark DeRosa had been hanging out with our bleacher section all three games before they went on the air. Thanking us for our hospitality, they watched Ramirez who had homered earlier off Lester, stand in against Chapman.

Ramirez fouled off a fastball, then swung and missed.

Everyone was on his or her feet screaming. Chapman threw. Ramirez swung, tipped the ball, and Willson Contreras hung on.

Cubs win! "Go Cubs Go" rang out on the diamond and streets of Wrigleyville. More "W" flags than I had ever seen were held up. The Cubs had won a World Series game at Wrigley Field for the first time since Game 6 in 1945.

It was a happy occasion, but as I noted earlier, bittersweet. The Wrigley Field 2016 season had ended. Hugs were exchanged between fans who'd known each other for years, would keep in touch over the winter, but might not see each other till April; the same were given to ballpark employees who'd been so helpful all spring, summer and fall.

I always linger a bit before leaving the ballpark for the year. Usually, it's with sadness that another failed season was over. Not this time, not with the Cubs in the World Series, even with needing to win two more games before the ultimate prize was won.

Heading down Waveland to my car, I exchanged high-fives with smiling Chicago police officers. The Cubs, at last, had brought joy to Wrigleyville in my lifetime.

Things got crazier before Game 6 even began. I'd been doing radio and TV spots talking Cubs with various local outlets, including WGN Radio and Fox-32 TV, but now the requests were coming from stations far afield. Pregame 6, I spoke to sports radio talk hosts in Toledo, Ohio—Indians country, even though the Triple-A team that plays there is affiliated with the Tigers—and EON Sports Radio, a national radio show in Australia, based in Melbourne.

The Cubs had become a worldwide story.

And Joe Maddon made the story even bigger pregame by tweaking his lineup—the Mad Scientist in Joe striking again. From 1 to 4, the lineup had read: Dexter Fowler, Kris Bryant, Anthony Rizzo, and Ben Zobrist for most of the second half of the year and into the postseason.

But with Kyle Schwarber now available, Joe apparently wanted to get him as many at-bats as possible, so he inserted Kyle in the No. 2 spot and moved everyone else down one.

Schwarber, though, was one of two easy outs recorded by Josh Tomlin in the first inning of Game 6. Then Bryant decided to begin to make this game one of his own. Bryant gave the Cubs a 1-0 lead with a 433-foot home run with two out in the first, a blast that might have hit the video board had it been at Wrigley Field.

The Cubs weren't done in that inning, either. Rizzo and Zobrist singled, and that brought Addison Russell to the plate. He hit what looked like a routine fly ball to right-center field.

Indians outfielders Tyler Naquin and Lonnie Chisenhall converged on the ball—and both ran right by it! It dropped for a double. Rizzo scored easily, and Zobrist bowled over catcher Roberto Perez in a scene we rarely see these days. The ball got away from Perez, but Zobrist likely would have been ruled safe anyway as Perez didn't give him a lane, as is now required under new rules intended to protect catchers from injury.

3-0 Cubs before Jake Arrieta even took the mound! And Jake was dealing, at times throwing as fast as 97 miles per hour, likely knowing he could leave everything on the Progressive Field mound in his last game of the year. And in the third inning, the Cubs blew the game open. Schwarber walked, and Rizzo and Zobrist again singled, loading the bases.

Russell took two pitches out of the zone. On the TV broadcast, John Smoltz had just finished saying how Tomlin was going to work Russell outside when Tomlin put a sinker right in the middle of the zone.

Boom! Grand slam, 7-0 Cubs lead! The significant minority of Cubs fans at Progressive Field were audible, loudly, on the TV broadcast.

Jason Kipnis ended any thought of Jake throwing a no-hitter with a leadoff double in the fourth. He eventually scored to make it 7-1, and in the next inning, homered to make it 7-2. Throughout the series, Kipnis crushed Cubs pitching. Fortunately, in this game it only gave the Indians fans a brief time to cheer and didn't affect the final result.

Jake made it through two out in the sixth—I thought he could have gone farther, but of course I'll defer to Joe Maddon's expertise—and Mike Montgomery finished off that inning, getting a slick play by Russell and Javier Baez on a ground-ball forceout at second.

In the seventh with two out, after Montgomery had allowed a walk and a single, Joe called on Aroldis Chapman. That sent Twitter ablaze with commentary, but again, Joe generally knows best.

Chapman got out of the inning on two pitches. He covered first on a grounder to Rizzo, and at first Francisco Lindor was called safe. Replay review showed Chapman's spike touching first base literally an instant before Lindor's. out!

This was a more important out than it might have at first seemed. If Lindor's safe, the bases are loaded and Mike Napoli is at the plate.

On the game went to the eighth. The Cubs went down, and Chapman came out again, even though he had appeared to tweak his ankle on the seventh-inning play. Apparently physically healthy, Chapman allowed a one-out single before Russell and Baez again combined on a sparkling defensive play, starting an inning-ending double play.

Despite getting past "five outs" in the NLCS clincher easily, that barrier was still making some fans a bit edgy in Game 6 of the World Series. It was nice to get past it with two outs on one play.

The Cubs tacked on two runs in the ninth on a majestic home run by Anthony Rizzo, his first of the World Series. With a six-run lead, the Cubs apparently would not need Chapman to go farther—they'd need to save as much of his heat as possible for Game 7.

Yet there he was, throwing to the leadoff hitter in the ninth, Brandon Guyer, who walked. Maddon, later explained that he didn't think Pedro Strop was quite ready to go at the top of the inning given the quick explosion of Rizzo's homer.

Strop came in, wild-pitched Guyer to second and then Perez laced a double down the right-field line. Guyer scored, but Jason Heyward showed the reason why he's in the lineup (as he had earlier in the game with a diving catch off the bat of Jose Ramirez). He threw out Perez trying to take second base—and credit Russell with a nice swipe tag. Maybe he's learning this sort of thing from Baez!

Another walk brought Travis Wood into the game, and a foul popup ended it, and the World Series was tied.

Three games each. It couldn't have been much closer at this point: 20 runs for the Indians, 19 for the Cubs. Each team took a game by one run. The Cubs won a game by four runs and one by six; the Indians had a six-run victory and a five-run victory.

One of these teams would end a decades-long, or longer, title drought in Game 7.

During the entire postseason, every now and again, a song kept popping into my head. It was "Tonight, Tonight" by the Smashing

Pumpkins—a group headed by Chicago native and Cubs fan Billy Corgan. The lyrics of that song resonated with me as a Cubs fan.

Beyond that, though . . . this song only came into my head on nights the Cubs won during the postseason. You can believe that or not, as you wish, but I swear it's true. On the six nights they lost, I did not have that earworm.

All day Wednesday, November 2, I kept hearing those words, those lyrics, that song going through my head. Somehow, I knew the Cubs would win Game 7.

The emotions of every single person who is a Cubs fan took an unbelievable roller-coaster ride during Game 7. The Cubs' early lead on Dexter Fowler's home run and Kris Bryant's daring baserunning. The errors and over-managing by Joe Maddon that helped lead to a two-run wild pitch (talk about history, that hadn't happened since 1911) and eventually, a two-run homer by Rajai Davis off Aroldis Chapman, who appeared to be going on fumes after 62 pitches thrown over two of the previous three days.

The Cubs had led this game 5–1 going into the bottom of the fifth and 6–3 going into the bottom of the eighth. Cubs history was littered with postseason games with leads this large, or even larger, blown, games and series lost.

This wouldn't, couldn't be another one. Could it?

Not for this team. If Game 7 didn't have enough going for it already, after the ninth inning ended tied, it started raining hard enough for the grounds crew to put the tarp on the field. The delay lasted a brief 17 minutes, but that was long enough for Jason Heyward to call a quick team meeting to remind everyone that they'd come this far, won this many games, to complete the journey.

Jason Heyward, who struggled all year at the plate (though providing strong outfield defense), might have made his biggest contribution to the team with that meeting.

Whether it did something or not is for the players to say and for history to decide, but the 10th-inning rally came right after that and it's certainly worth reliving in detail. Kyle Schwarber singled, concluding a magical World Series in which he went 7-for-17 (.412) after no one thought he'd play until 2017. Albert Almora Jr. ran for him and alertly tagged up and took second on a fly out. That left first base open, and Anthony Rizzo was intentionally walked.

Ben Zobrist, who played a key role in the World Series title of the 2015 Royals, was next, and he rose to the occasion with a run-scoring double, sending Rizzo to third.

With another base open, Addison Russell was intentionally walked. That filled the bases and brought up Miguel Montero, a somewhat-forgotten man much of the second half, so much so he feared the Cubs might release him.

Montero bounced a run-scoring single up the middle and the Cubs led by two. That run would turn out to be very, very important.

Carl Edwards Jr. entered the game to try to save it, and the World Series title, for the Cubs. The skinny right-hander, who can throw 95-plus, struck out the powerful Mike Napoli and got Jose Ramirez to ground to second.

Two out—one more to go!

Then he walked Brandon Guyer, who then took second because the Cubs weren't holding him.

Davis was up next. Gulp. Davis singled and Guyer scored and it was 8–7.

Joe Maddon came out for another pitching change. The previous two in this game hadn't worked out so well. Gulp.

Mike Montgomery entered to pitch to Michael Martinez, who had been inserted by the Indians for defense an inning earlier.

Montgomery got a curveball across for strike one.

His second curveball was hit, slowly, toward Kris Bryant who charged the ball and made a strong and accurate throw to Anthony Rizzo. When the ball nestled into Rizzo's glove, the smile wider on his face than any Cub's in 108 years, the Chicago Cubs were World Series champions.

I celebrated quietly at home, but not long after the game, I stepped out on my deck just to get some air. It was well past midnight in Chicago. I live about 2½ miles from Wrigley Field. I could hear the cheering in Wrigleyville from my deck, hear horns honking and fireworks going off, and realized this was a celebration 108 years in the making. The city was still buzzing the morning after, as I lined up with others at a local 7-Eleven to get extra copies of the local newspapers commemorating this historic happening.

The Cubs are World Series champions. I wrote those words at the beginning of this chapter and I have to write them again because I figure the more I write them and read them, the more real they will be. It really did happen, in my lifetime, seeing something I once never thought I'd see.

This, of course, is the end of this year's story, the culmination of a long, long journey. Let's go back to the beginning—the very beginning, right after the Cubs last won the World Series.

Chapter One

How the Cubs Got Here

Wednesday, October 14, 1908, was a pleasant, mild day in Detroit, Michigan, with the temperature in the upper 60s.

And yet, just 6,210 people paid to watch Game 5 of the World Series between the Cubs and Tigers. It's the smallest crowd for any game in World Series history.

The Cubs won the game, 2–0, behind Orval Overall, and though that sounds like a made-up name, it's not. Overall's three-hit shutout won the Series for the Cubs, four games to one. The win made the Cubs the first team to win consecutive World Series.

I could go through the litany of things that have happened in the 108 years since, but you've probably heard them all before, and likely too many times, from national media who stick to an old, tired narrative. (Raise your hand if you've heard a national TV announcer, doing a Cubs game, say, "The Cubs haven't won the World Series since 1908"—proudly, as if he's stating a fact that no one's ever heard before.) There is one fact regarding the Cubs' 107-year drought that stands out to me, though. And that is, until this year's triumph, there was no radio call of a Cubs World Series title . . . because commercial radio was still 12 years from existing when the 1908 championship was won.

So, Pat Hughes, congratulations to you, too. You're the first radio announcer ever to say on the air, "The Cubs are World Series champions!"

Every one of the 6,210 people who watched that game in Detroit in 1908 is deceased. No, I haven't checked, but I'm reasonably certain there weren't any small children there who might be living today because in 1908, attending ball games wasn't a thing kids generally did. Even at that, you'd have to be very old now to have been at that game, and probably too young to remember the event. So I think it's safe to say that before 2016, there hadn't been a living person to witness the Cubs winning the World Series, likely in decades.

Every one of the players who took part in that game is deceased. The last living Cub who played in that World Series, pitcher Ed Reulbach, died fifty-five years ago, in 1961.

And yet, at the time that World Series—the third consecutive Series the Cubs had played in—was won, everyone in baseball likely thought the Cubs would continue their dominance. They'd been the best team in the game for those seasons. Catcher Johnny Kling sat out the entire 1909 season because he thought he'd make more money running a pool hall in his hometown of Kansas City than playing baseball, a quaint notion in our time of multimillion-dollar contracts. If not for that, the Cubs might have won five straight pennants, because Kling's replacements were awful. Even so, the 1909 Cubs won 104 games, the most ever by a second-place team (matched only by the 1942 Dodgers).

The pennant in 1910, marked by a World Series loss to the A's, signaled the end of Cubs dominance in that era. And that's not uncommon in baseball—teams' success ebbs and flows, teams go through periods of winning, and as players get older and are replaced by lesser ones, a period of decline occurs. That was as true in the 2010s as in the 1910s.

Still, the Cubs moved on through the years, winning a sort of "rump" pennant in 1918, a year when the season was shortened due to World War I, and there were rumblings of gambling and game-fixing before the Black Sox scandal eventually blew the lid off that all around baseball. They eventually built a winning team in the 1920s under the then-progressive ownership of William Wrigley that lasted nearly a decade and four pennants' worth, every three years like proverbial clockwork from 1929–38, and eking out one final National League flag in 1945, more than a decade after Bill Wrigley had died and his son P.K. Wrigley had inherited the team, supposedly telling his father on the elder's deathbed that he'd never sell the Cubs.

In 1945, the Cubs would have been seen as one of the premier franchises in NL history. They'd won 10 pennants in the previous 40 seasons, and two World Series titles. Between 1900 and 1945, only one other NL team had done anything like that: the Giants (13 pennants, four World Series).

And then: nothing. The reasons are well known: poor ownership and management by the Wrigleys, whose time had likely passed by the time World War II ended, and teams that got close only to suffer soul-crushing collapses or defeats. There was the wacky College of Coaches idea that only made the team worse, followed by Leo Durocher's managerial style that was more suited to the 1940s than the 1960s and the cultural change that was then happening. Management spent money on free agents in the 1990s, but seemingly never wisely. Sammy Sosa and his home runs brought excitement and helped bring the Cubs to the postseason twice, but never a title.

The 1969 team, the one that's beloved five decades later despite never winning anything, is another example of just how long this drought was before 2016. In 1969, it had been 24 years since the last pennant, 61 since the last World Championship.

It's a sobering thought that as of this year, the drought of not even getting to the World Series became ten years longer than the title drought was in 1969. People fresh out of college in 1969 who fell in love with that team and figured, "Hey, this team is still young enough, they can do it next year," are now collecting Social Security.

The failures of 1984 and 2003 are still too raw for many of us to discuss here, and that's not the purpose of this book, which is to celebrate the championship that we have all been waiting for, that many of our elders lived and died and never saw. But the reality of baseball life is that the Cubs probably were good enough to have won the World Series several times since 1908.

The 1929 team was probably the best in the interim, winning 98 games. Only one Cubs team (1935) won more than that since then, before this year. They scored 982 runs in '29, which I consider a more impressive feat than the 998 they scored the following year, which was only second in the offensively-charged 1930 season, when the entire NL batted .303. The '29 team should probably have defeated the A's in the World Series, but that year might have been a harbinger of what Lou Piniella eventually called "Cubbie Occurrences."

Trailing two games to one in the Series, the Cubs had an 8–0 lead in the seventh inning of Game 4. Hack Wilson lost two balls in the late-afternoon sun, the latter going for an inside-the-park three-run homer, and the A's' 10-run inning stunned the Cubs. Two days later, the Cubs took a 2–0 lead into the bottom of the ninth in Game 5, but pitcher Pat Malone gave up a two-run homer and then two more hits won the game, and the Series, for the Athletics.

In 1935, the Cubs, sitting in third place in early September with a good 79–52 record but 2 1/2 games out of first place, ran off 21 straight wins, the longest winning streak in big-league history, clinching the pennant with a doubleheader sweep of the Cardinals that culminated that streak (they lost the season's final two games after that). They won 100 games, the last time before 2016 that any Cubs team hit the century mark in victories, seven more regular-season wins than the AL champion Tigers. But Detroit, who'd lost the previous year's series to St. Louis, won three straight after the Cubs won Game 1, and though the Cubs forced a Game 6 by taking Game 5 at Wrigley, they blew a sixth-inning lead in that sixth game and lost the game and series in Detroit, perhaps a measure of Detroit revenge for the 1908 result.

The 1984 Cubs might not have won the World Series, but they surely would have given the Tigers better competition than the Padres, who seemed happy just to be there. As someone who attended NLCS Games 4 and 5 in San Diego, I can attest to the fact that the fans there treated Cubs fans just brutally. They appeared happier that the Cubs lost than that their team won.

Most of the other Cubs postseason teams in the divisional-play era probably weren't good enough to win it all. In 1989, the Cubs made it to the playoffs as much in spite of Don Zimmer's managing as because of it; the 1998 wild-card team spent all their energy just getting there and were no match for the Braves; and in 2007, Piniella's decision to "save" Carlos Zambrano for a Game 4 that never happened probably cost the team Game 1, and eventually the series, when Big Z was lifted despite dominating the Diamondbacks. Cubs fans were a significant presence at Chase Field, but they lost both there and at Wrigley to Arizona, a sweep that made for six straight postseason defeats.

Which leaves 2003 and 2008.

Of 2003, we should probably speak no more in this book. The "incident," and I shall call it nothing more, has been way overdone by the national media and isn't the reason the Cubs lost the NLCS to the Marlins.

The 2008 season . . . now, there's a puzzle. That year's Cubs blew through the NL Central and peaked at 35 games over .500 (85–50), the most games over the break-even mark since 1945. They'd done other things that hadn't been done since the 1930s, including 855 runs, the most since 1930.

When fans entered Wrigley Field on October 1, 2008, though, the atmosphere wasn't like a playoff game. It was almost funereal, weird, quiet. Most regular bleacher fans and season-ticket holders noticed. Talk was that many die-hard fans had sold their NLDS tickets and kept their World Series tickets in anticipation . . . of something that never happened.

I won't blame the atmosphere on the Game 1 loss; Ryan Dempster simply didn't have command and issued seven walks, including walking the bases loaded in the fifth inning. The Cubs had a 2–0 lead and Dempster was one strike away from getting out of the jam, at which time the bullpen could have taken over.

But James Loney hit a grand slam off Dempster, the Cubs lost 7–2, and the next day all four infielders made errors on the way to a 10–3 Dodgers win. The third loss, 3–1 at Dodger Stadium two days later, was just a formality, and the playoff losing streak reached nine.

And that's why the 2015 season felt like such a gift. The 2008 team faded, with general manager Jim Hendry pulling several last-gasp moves to try to help that core to one more playoff appearance, only to make the club worse and get himself fired.

That brought in Theo Epstein to run baseball operations. It's again a sobering thought to wonder where the Cubs would be now if the Red Sox hadn't blown a ninth-inning lead in the final regular-season game in 2011. If Boston makes the playoffs that year and has a long postseason run, do they keep Theo?

Epstein ripped the big-league team apart and built a system fresh from the bottom up. He had to. The Hendry regime hadn't left much behind in the minor leagues. Some fans wanted that win-now attitude to start with Theo's first year, but in hindsight, he absolutely did the right thing, and the bad years from 2012–14 helped bring Kris Bryant and Kyle Schwarber, among others, to the team by draft. Shrewd trades brought Jake Arrieta and Anthony Rizzo into the fold.

Still, the earliest some people thought the team would contend was 2016, even with the signing of the 2014–15 offseason's top free-agent pitcher, Jon Lester, and having had an excellent manager, Joe Maddon, dropped in their laps. Instead, they muddled around .500 until late July, when they were no-hit by Cole Hamels in his final Phillies start, breaking an MLB-record streak of 7,920 consecutive games with at least one hit, dating back to Sandy Koufax's perfect game in 1965.

After Hamels's gem, the Cubs went on an historic run, going 46–20, by far the best record in baseball, helped along by Arrieta, who won the Cy Young Award and had a second-half mark that hadn't been done by a pitcher since the pre-1920 Deadball Era: 20 starts with an 0.86 ERA and 0.701 WHIP, and as many home runs hit (two) as allowed. They finished just three games behind the Cardinals, in third place with 97 wins, the best third-place record in major-league history.

Schwarber smashed a colossal home run that landed in the Allegheny River past the right-field seats at PNC Park, and Arrieta dispatched the Pirates in the wild-card game with a complete-game shutout, the team's first postseason win since Game 4 of the 2003 NLCS. Then the first-ever playoff series between the Cubs and Cardinals, ancient rivals, featured a game with a postseason-record six homers by the Cubs, and another game where a ball was deposited on top of the right-field video board by Schwarber, a feat commemorated with a 2016 bobblehead, even though Schwarber's horrifying April injury put him out until the World Series.

I'm one of those fans scarred by the 1969 Mets' comeback to take the NL East title away from a Cubs team we thought should have won it all. For years I despised the Mets, even after the Cubs took a division title away from them in 1984—it wasn't quite the same because the Cubs didn't win the World Series, as the 1969 Mets had. That hatred quieted for a time when baseball's mid-1990s realignment put the teams in different divisions.

And then there they were, the two old rivals, playing in the National League Championship Series in 2015. Could this exorcise the ghosts of 1969? Of course the players are different, and two generations of fans have grown up since then. Some of us, though, wanted revenge, to heal our broken childhood hearts.

It didn't happen, but you know what? I don't hate the Mets quite as much as I did back in '69. They defeated the Cubs fair and square in that four-game sweep in October 2015. They pitched better and hit better. They were just a superior team, at least for those four games, a different club than the Cubs had swept in seven regular-season games earlier that year.

The ghosts are gone, for me at least. The Cubs had been built to win soon but didn't quite scale the mountain in 2015. But it wasn't a 1969-style collapse. They just got beat.

But 2016. Now that would be different, as the Cubs went out and signed free agents Jason Heyward, Ben Zobrist, and John Lackey, and the young core led by Bryant and Rizzo had playoff experience. They'd be a target. Maddon, to help his players (and fans) combat this, invented a slogan, "Embrace the Target," that wound up on T-shirts sold to benefit his foundation.

Before I relate the tale of the 2016 champion Cubs, let me tell you the story of how I became the Cubs fan I am today.

Chapter Two

One Fan's Journey

Saturday, July 6, 1963, was a pleasant, sunny Chicago-area summer afternoon, typical for the time of year. The temperature peaked at 79 degrees, with light south winds, and no rain was in the forecast.

And so it was the perfect time for my dad to take me from our north suburban home to my first game at Wrigley Field.

Things then weren't like they are now. The Cubs had been mediocre-to-awful for 16 seasons, never having a winning year in that span, and were coming off a franchise-record 103-loss season in 1962.

You didn't have to wonder about "dynamic pricing" or StubHub fees for Cubs games back then. Even with the 1963 Cubs playing better than the previous year's edition—they had briefly been in first place in June and were just three games back entering the action on July 6—grandstand tickets were freely available and cost just $1.50. For adults, that is! For a child under 14—that would have been me, by a considerable margin, in 1963—it cost just 60 cents to get into Wrigley Field. (That's $11.82 and $4.73, respectively, in 2016, according to the U.S. Government's inflation calculator, just a tiny bit less than you'd actually pay for similar seats in the season just completed.)

Hot dogs cost 30 cents, pop 25 cents, and an Old Style beer was just 40 cents. It was a simpler time, a time where the Wrigleys still put 22,000 unreserved seats on sale the morning of every game, 3,300 of them in the bleachers, the rest in what we'd now call "Terrace Box" or "Terrace Reserved," then simply called "Grandstand." Jack Brickhouse would often shill for people to "Come on down!" and buy one of these seats on TV. Thousands of them would go unsold most days in the low years of 1946–66. It got so bad that between 1959 and 1966, there were nine paid "crowds" of less than 1,000. Four of those were fewer than 600, a number that could comfortably fit into a couple of sections of the newly reconstructed Wrigley bleachers.

But on that summer 1963 afternoon, my dad and I settled into two of those unreserved grandstand seats and watched the Cubs get shut out by the Phillies, 6–0, getting just two hits, and the pitcher who threw the shutout was someone the Cubs had discarded over a decade earlier, the charmingly named Calvin Coolidge Julius Caesar Tuskahoma McLish. The attendance, on a gorgeous Saturday afternoon, to see a good Cubs team (45–35, in second place, three games out of first place entering that day's action): 16,348, less than half the venerable ballpark's seats filled.

And that was how I began my indoctrination to decades of Cubs failure, and one reason this year's World Series win is so much sweeter.

Of course, because I was living in the suburbs, it wasn't practical nor easy to get to many games while I was still in elementary school. But that's where the magic of WGN-TV came in. Since the station went on the air in 1948—just weeks before a FCC station-license freeze would have made them wait five more years—they had televised every Cubs home game, a perfect two or three hours' worth of programming in a fledgling industry with every channel looking for material to fill their airtime.

It did more than fill the hours, even though the team was bad. With games starting at 1:30, kids coming home from school shortly after 3 p.m. could watch the Cubs every spring, summer, and fall afternoon. It created several generations' worth of Cubs fans, from Chicagoans in the 1950s, 1960s, and 1970s to a nationwide audience once WGN-TV went on national cable in the 1980s and 1990s.

I was nearly seven years old in the summer of 1963, the perfect age to be exposed to baseball, both in person, on television, and in the neighborhood playing the game with friends. Like many my age, I had several years' worth of baseball cards from that era thrown out by well-meaning parents who thought the closet space could be better used. Sure, they'd be worth plenty now, but if everyone whose parents tossed their cards kept them . . . well, the value wouldn't be anything close to what it is now.

So I spent those formative years of becoming a baseball fan watching Jack Brickhouse and his sidekicks, Vince Lloyd (later moved to radio after the tragic death of WGN radio announcer Jack Quinlan in a car accident) and Lloyd Pettit, call games of Cubs teams who never really had a chance to win. But sunny Jack was always optimistic! If only a bounce could go this way instead of the other, or a pitcher not get hit the way he was, or an error not be made . . . why, this might be the year the Cubs finally get out of the doldrums. If they lost, they were "snakebit" or came up "a day late and a dollar short."

In this more cynical modern age, an announcer like Brickhouse might be laughed off the air. But those were simpler times, and Brickhouse became the soundtrack to my childhood, pleasant afternoons spent watching the Cubs on a gigantic Zenith black-and-white television that had a screen with rounded corners that seemed as if it took up half the living room.

It was the perfect time to become a Cubs fan, and I was the perfect age to fall in love with this team for life. The tween years—ages about nine to 12—are formative years for many attachments but somewhat too early for interest in the opposite sex. It's a time when you are playing sports, learning the games' rules, and studying up about the pros who play the sport you love best. It's not too much of an exaggeration to say that batting averages, ERAs, and similar stats helped me learn math concepts in elementary school.

School friends and I would play a game outside my elementary school we called "lineball," but it was also known in other parts of the Chicago area as "fastball" or "fastpitch," where just two kids made up entire teams. One would stand next to a box painted on a brick wall of the school made to denote a strike zone, the other would pitch. Depending on how far (and where) you'd hit the ball—generally a tennis ball—it was a single, double, triple, or home run. At my school there was a fence just far enough so that an eight- or nine-year-old kid could hit home runs over the fence, but not too many, which made for competitive games. One particular friend of mine was a Dodgers fan, so I spent many happy afternoons there pretending to be Ron Santo or Ernie Banks, while taking pitches from him pretending to be Sandy Koufax or Don Drysdale.

Those ages for me were also the era of the heyday of the team of Banks, Santo, Billy Williams, and Fergie Jenkins, Hall of Famers all. That team wasn't very good at the beginning of that time in my life, but they suddenly broke free of 20 years of nonwinning records and climbed into first place July 2, 1967, with a doubleheader sweep of the Reds. It was the first time the Cubs had been in first place that late in the year since 1945, and the raucous full house at Wrigley Field simply refused to leave what the Chicago Tribune called the "ancient" park until the scoreboard operator changed the order of the flags that depict the current standings to show the Cubs on top.

I was not quite 11. The Cubs were my first love.

And two years later, they broke my heart, and the hearts of millions of Cubs fans, by blowing a nine-game lead in August and collapsing to the Mets, who became despised by generations of Cubs fans. There was an eight-game losing streak involved, but the most painful of all of the losses happened September 7, 1969, at Wrigley Field. I was at that game. It happens to be the earliest-surviving scorecard in my collection. With two out and two strikes on Willie Stargell and the Cubs leading 5–4 in the top of the ninth, Cubs closer Phil Regan served up a ball that Stargell parked on Sheffield, and the game was tied. The Cubs lost on an error in the 11th. To this day, that's one of the saddest happenings in Cubs history.

But hey! The optimistic 13-year-old in me thought, "This is a really good team! They'll win it next year!"

But "next year," 1970, came and went, with the Cubs again rolling out to a lead in June, only to fade. The phrase "June swoon" became a mantra for Cubs fans in the early 1970s.

And the next year, and the next, and the next... Then in 1973, another collapse, an eight-game lead in late June, and a 48–33 mark turned into a 29–51 second half and a potential late-September comeback lost, again to the hated Mets, on a miserable 40-degree day on the Monday after the season was supposed to end, in front of just 1,913 fans. Just five paid crowds since then have been smaller.

After that year, that core of beloved players was broken up, traded away, every one of them (except Ernie, too cherished, who was allowed to retire gracefully with the team) when management "backed up the truck"—almost literally: WGN-TV did a preseason special in 1974 with that title, with video of a cargo truck with its back open backing up to Wrigley Field—and started over.

It was just around that time that I discovered the pleasures of the Wrigley Field bleachers.

Since I was living in the suburbs, it wasn't easy to get to Wrigley until I was considered "old enough" to get on the old Chicago & North Western (now part of "Metra") train, change trains in Evanston, and take the L to the ballpark. In the year 2016 you wouldn't think of letting an eighth-grader do that unsupervised, but at 13 I did that several times, along with a group of friends, and we sat in the grandstand mostly.

The bleachers were a foreign place filled with yellow-hard-hatted "Bums" who blasted noise from horns and not considered a safe spot for kids by some. In reality, the Bleacher Bums were a pleasant, welcoming group and surely would have been kind to young teenage Cubs fans. The bleacher fans who are now among my best friends are the Bums' descendants, not literally, but certainly in spirit.

So it wasn't until 1974, the year before I left Chicago for college (of course, I returned after graduation), that I started spending significant time in the bleachers. In one of the first games I sat out there, I wasn't aware of the concept of "sunscreen" and got a horrific sunburn. Later I went to a game in which Davey Lopes hit three homers against the Cubs and the first one nearly hit me in the head as I arrived just as the game started.

Then there were the 1977 Cubs, who went out to a 47–22 start. There was a popular rock song that year, by Southside Johnny and the Asbury Jukes, titled "This Time It's for Real." That song became my anthem that hot and sticky summer; surely, this time the Cubs would win it all, for real. They reached that 25-over-.500 mark in a win over the Expos in Montreal that wasn't televised. (Yes, kids, there was once a time where not every Cubs game was on TV.) So I listened to that one on WGN radio and heard analyst Lou Boudreau, on the postgame show, enthuse: "They can kiss the .500 mark goodbye!"

The joke, of course, among the gallows humor that all Cubs fans learned by rote in those days, is that team finished 81–81, exactly .500, and they had to lose their last five games to do it.

I wound up sitting in various places in the bleachers until, during the offseason of 1978–79, I answered an ad placed in the Chicago Reader. No, not for a job—this was placed by disgruntled Cubs fans calling themselves Chicagoans United for a Baseball Series (you see the acronym, of course). The avowed goal of this group was to get the Wrigleys to sell the Cubs. They created a logo with a backwards "C"—like an upside-down flag, it was supposed to be a symbol of distress.

It was through this "organization" (it disbanded after a summer of holding up signs in the bleachers, nearly having it stolen in St. Louis, and making up T-shirts) that I met a group of bleacher fans who dated back all the way to the beginnings of Wrigley Field in 1916. One of the last of the old-timers was Carl Leone, known to all as "Papa Carl." A retired industrial paint sprayer, Carl took pride in arriving before everyone else to the day-of-game bleacher ticket line, where he'd buy ticket no. 0001 every day. (He gave me a stack of those No. 1 tickets one day. I still have every single one of them.)

Carl introduced me and some of my newfound friends in C.U.B.S. to team and Wrigley lore, including having watched Babe Ruth play at Wrigley in the 1932 World Series. Another Wrigley event caused Carl's glass eye. He'd been hit in the eye by a batting-practice home run sometime in the mid-1970s, a few years before I met him. After that he was always more careful during BP.

Sadly, I only got to hang with Carl for a year or so. His wife passed away in 1980, and that took something out of him that he never got back. He didn't come to the park after that and died in 1985.

But four of us—me, Mike, Dave, and Phil—who began sitting together in 1979 (Mike and Dave were part of this group for several years before that) carry on the traditions of bleacher fans who go back to the beginnings of Wrigley more than 100 years ago. We're still together in the bleachers, although in a different location, caused by the reconfiguration of the bleachers after the 2005–06 reconstruction. Our original seating area was gone in the new seating configuration; we've made the left-field corner our new home.

And so my bleacher fandom continued through the addition of lights, seasons in which the Cubs got thisclose to the ultimate goal that's at last been reached, other seasons in which my friends and I had our bleacher section to ourselves as 95 or more losses were recorded.

Beyond the bleachers, I often traveled the country when it was possible for the Cubs to clinch a postseason spot, or even get to the World Series.

In 1984, when living Cubs fans under the age of about 50 wouldn't have had any clear memory of the team in the postseason, I drove to St. Louis on the penultimate weekend of the season hoping to see them clinch the NL East there.

They lost the Friday game, 8–0—their fifth straight loss. Even though the team's magic number had been reduced to three, those of us who had lived through the heartbreak of 1969 got a bit nervous. The Saturday game was rained out, forcing a doubleheader Sunday, which the Cubs swept.

But the Mets won their weekend games, as well, meaning the Cubs would have to head to Pittsburgh for their next shot at clinching the division.

I had to see it. I drove back to Chicago at a speed—well, let's just say that speed would be legal now—and got myself on a flight to Pittsburgh. Sort of. In those early days of airline deregulation, there was an airline known as People Express, which would fly you cheaply anywhere, as long as you changed planes in Newark. So off I went to Newark, then Pittsburgh, where about 5,000 fans— almost all Cubs fans—cheered on the Cubs to a 4–1 division-clinching win, led by Cy Young winner Rick Sutcliffe. We stayed in Three Rivers Stadium as the Pirates posted a congratulatory graphic on their video board—and then showed, via video from Chicago, the celebrations in the streets outside Wrigley.

Back in Chicago, the Cubs still had to finish a few regular-season games, including the season-ender against the rival Cardinals. The last game of the year went into the bottom of the ninth with St. Louis up, 1–0, with ex-Cub Bruce Sutter going for what would have been a then-record-breaking 46th save.

The Cubs won the game, 2–1, and on a day that was sunny but unseasonably chilly (I had to buy a "1984 NL East Champions" sweatshirt, which I still have, because temperatures were only in the 40s), no one left the park.

Ten minutes after game's end, the entire team came back on the field, some dressed in T-shirts, sweatpants, and shower clogs, to take a victory lap.

You might not think that's anything special, but sports teams, for the most part, didn't do that in 1984. It was a unique and special moment in Cubs history that I will always cherish.

Earlier that same day, I still needed one playoff ticket I hadn't obtained—to Game 1 of the NLCS. I ran into a friend of mine outside the ballpark before the game and mentioned this to him. He said, "Try the box office."

Again, this isn't something you could do in 2016, but I went up to the ticket windows and asked if they had any bleacher tickets for Game 1.

"How many do you want?" was the response.

I was so floored that I said, "Uh . . . just one." And that's how I saw Sutcliffe's homer that led the Cubs to a 13–0 win in Game 1, the ball flying right over my head in the right-field bleachers and onto Sheffield Avenue. The Game 2 win wasn't quite as easy, but the Cubs needed only one win to go to the World Series.

So I went to San Diego. Not one of you Cubs fans reading this wants to rehash that crushing loss; I'll simply say that Padres fans weren't very friendly, seemingly happier that the Cubs lost than that their team won, and when I went back to work the day after Game 5, more than one coworker said to me, "You look like someone in your family just died."

Well, yeah. Yeah. That's exactly how that felt.

I took similar trips for other Cubs playoff series. In 1989, I met Cubs pitcher Jeff Pico's parents in the parking lot at Candlestick Park. Pico never pitched for the Cubs in the postseason, but his folks, who lived in nearby Antioch, California, just wanted to be part of the atmosphere. So did I, even when the Cubs lost. Giants fans were much friendlier than Padres fans had been five years earlier, complimenting Mark Grace on his incredible NLCS performance (.647, 11-for-17, eight RBI, still not enough to bring the Cubs a series win).

The 1998 season, the Cubs' next playoff appearance, came in the wake of the Sammy Sosa/Mark McGwire home-run chase, the chase that later became tainted by PED accusations, and for the last 45 days of the season no team among the Cubs, Mets, and Giants led that wild-card race by more than one game. I rarely go to bars to watch games, but friends invited me to a gathering in one of the watering holes across from Wrigley to watch the final regular-season game that the Cubs wound up losing to the Astros. They'd still need the Giants to lose to force a wild-card tiebreaker. Not 30 seconds after the Cubs' loss, future Cub Neifi Perez hit a walk-off homer for the Rockies to defeat the Giants.

I left the bar to the sight of literally hundreds of people running down the middle of Clark Street toward the ticket windows to buy tickets for the next day's tiebreaker game. In today's sanitized, online-only ticket marketplace, you'd never see that happening. Pity, really; I only wish the smartphone era had begun a few years earlier so I could have shot video of that scene.

When Grace squeezed former Cub No. 1 draft pick Joe Carter's popup to win the wild-card game (it was, in fact, the final at-bat of Carter's career), I said to Dave, regarding the entire season, "If they don't win another game, it was all worth it."

That's exactly what happened. The Braves swept the Cubs out of the postseason, winning the division series three games to none—but the 1998 season was indeed worth it, every moment, even with the cloud of PED suspicion.

The events of 2003 are too sad to recount in this book, especially considering the triumph we have just witnessed. I had wanted to see the Cubs win the pennant so badly that I'd bought extra tickets for the games in Miami, expecting friends to join me, and traveled there. The Marlins opened up the upper deck to the football stadium they then played in, and there were so many tickets available I couldn't find any takers. My friends and I found some worthy Cubs fans to take the tickets—for free, on the day of Game 5, the game we hoped would put the Cubs, with a 3–1 series lead, into the World Series.

It didn't—Carlos Zambrano had one of his then-rare bad games and no one was hitting Josh Beckett that day—and I got stuck halfway between tiers at the football stadium, since I thought I'd try to get down to the field level to celebrate the pennant, silly me. Later I met up with some friends for dinner, including my friend Jessica, who'd been seated next to a vice president of the

Hooters restaurant chain. He gave her some coupons for free food. So we commiserated the Cubs' loss at a random suburban Miami Hooters. The food was good, anyway.

The Cubs faded in 2005 and lost 96 games in 2006, after which they changed management at the executive level (John McDonough replacing Andy MacPhail) and on the field (Lou Piniella replacing Dusty Baker). And a change happened to me early in 2007 that would make that year, and all the years since, much more enjoyable, both personally and in my love for the Cubs. I met a woman who loved the Cubs and knew as much about them as I did.

Well, it didn't take long until Miriam and I were sharing a bleacher bench at Wrigley, and since 2007, we've also gone to Cubs games in Atlanta, Cincinnati, Phoenix, Toronto, Milwaukee, Washington, Philadelphia, Pittsburgh, New York, Arlington, Boston, Kansas City, Minneapolis, San Francisco, Oakland, and St. Louis, as well as side trips to the 2012 All-Star Game in Kansas City and a pilgrimage to Cooperstown, where we were supposed to see the final Hall of Fame Game in 2008, only to see it rained out.

It's been a wonderful journey together, but it was always missing something. Until November 2, 2016, the date that will be inscribed forever in every Cubs fan's book of baseball life as the date of our ultimate joy.

The 2016 journey began on a back field in Mesa, Arizona, on a sunny Thursday, February 25.

Chapter 3

Spring Training: The Preparation, the Sunshine, the Fun of March

Sloan Park, the Cubs' spring-training complex that replaced their former HoHoKam Park home in 2014, occupies about 25 acres of land on the western edge of Mesa, Arizona. It's hemmed in on the north by a freeway (Arizona Loop 202) and adjacent to a water-treatment plant that's been carefully painted and disguised so that if you didn't know what it was, you'd think it was part of the Cubs' complex. The complex's other neighbor is Maricopa County Animal Care and Control, immediately west of the Cubs' practice fields. The latter means that when you pull into the parking lot next to those fields, the first sounds you hear aren't of ball hitting bat, but of dozens of yelping dogs held in the county pound.

Those were the sounds that greeted me on February 25 as I arrived not only to watch the Cubs' first full-squad workout, but to take part in an interview with Cubs chairman Tom Ricketts along with several other Cubs bloggers.

While we were waiting for the meeting with Tom, we hung around watching the Cubs practice on several of the four fields that surround a tower where management can watch from all angles.

Suddenly, manager Joe Maddon gathered the entire squad on Field 6. Looking at the scene, I figured it was the right time for a team meeting, get all the guys together, give them one of the patented Maddon pep talks.

And then there was a commotion not 20 feet away from me. With all the kerfuffle going on, I didn't figure out what it was until I saw Dexter Fowler, in street clothes, walking toward the scrum on the pitchers' mound. It happened so fast that I didn't have a chance to get my phone out; otherwise, I'd have had close-up video of Fowler's unexpected return to the Cubs

Instead, what happened was that we bloggers who were waiting to talk to Tom Ricketts wound up sitting on some of the bleacher benches next to Field 3, frantically typing on the devices we'd brought to take interview notes in order to post stories on Dexter's surprise comeback to the Cubs. My eternal thanks to Neil Finnell of Chicago Cubs Online, whose Wi-Fi hotspot we all used in order to upload our dispatches from Mesa.

And that was just the first day of spring training! The rest of that day wasn't nearly as exciting, though seeing Tom Ricketts' enthusiasm for the upcoming season in our talk with him gave all of us new optimism coming off the 2015 postseason appearance. Among others, he said he told the players three key things:

- The most important people are the fans. Even understanding the time pressures players can be under with getting their work done, he wants them to spend a little extra time acknowledging fans, signing autographs, etc.
- He emphasized being professional "both on and off the field." Without mentioning any names or specific incidents, he referred in general to things that have happened with athletes in other sports and he wanted Cubs players to reflect well on the team and the organization. (This point would come into play later in the year again when the Cubs traded for Aroldis Chapman.)
- He asked players to give to the community, spending time in schools, hospitals, etc. Many Cubs players do this already, but Ricketts made the point that he wants them to do more.
- After that, it was off to watch drills.

Now, don't think I'm complaining, because being in gloriously sunny, 80-degree weather in Arizona in February is far preferable to slogging through snow piles and wind chills in Chicago.

But after you've watched about 20 minutes' worth of spring-training drills, you've pretty much seen all you're going to see. The players go through the same things over and over and over and over. They begin fielding practice of various types, throwing-to-base tries or whatever, then they go to the back of the line, and the coaches run them through the drill again. I took video of these drills, but only about a minute's worth of each, to post on Bleed Cubbie Blue, just to show everyone who can't make it to Mesa exactly what goes on there.

It's as monotonous as that paragraph makes them sound. Yet, they're perhaps the most important things the team will do all spring. It's an effort to give the players muscle memory, doing these things over and over and over and over so that when the situations come up during the season, they won't have to think while executing a play, it'll just happen. You see tough plays executed all the time on major-league fields during the season, and the players make it look easy. Trust me, it's not.

This sort of thing occurs every day for a couple of weeks before the paying customers enter Sloan Park and the nine other Cactus League venues for actual games. What was surprising about spring 2016 in particular was the number of people sitting around watching these drills. There were probably 200–300 people on the back fields on the west side of the complex—under shades thoughtfully installed by the Cubs over some aluminum bleachers—and maybe another 100 or so out in the sun on Field 1, which is just across the road from Sloan Park itself.

It's a testament to the Cubs' popularity that these many fans will come out just to watch pitchers field bunts, or practice the 3–1 putout, over and over and over and over. On the other hand, this is baseball at its purest, breaking it down to the beginnings of how players learn the game, and people can watch this for free. Some of these folks are Phoenix-area residents who grew up as Cubs fans elsewhere, now live in the Valley of the Sun, and take this time every early spring to watch the newest incarnation of their heroes. Some are vacationers who can't make it to Mesa when games are going on but want their baseball fix, so they're content to watch Cubs hitters mash baseballs out of a practice field.

And some obtain attention they hadn't planned on. One of those people was Peter Gesler. He got that surprise notoriety on the first day of pitcher and catcher workouts, a week before Fowler's sudden return. Kyle Schwarber was taking batting practice. I had driven over to the complex to watch early practice on February 17 and had pulled into a parking space in the lot just behind right field on Field 1. On opening my car door, I heard someone say to me, as if he were telling me a state secret, "You might not want to park there."

So I moved my car to the lot across the road and began walking toward the field. I'm grateful to that anonymous soul who suggested I move my car because it wasn't more than five minutes later that I heard a crunching noise. That was the sound of a baseball hit by Schwarber that cleared a 40-foot-high screen and hit Peter's windshield.

Peter, Kyle, the Cubs, and the Safelite windshield-repair company turned this incident into a fun promotion. Safelite fixed Peter's windshield for free, and Kyle posed for photos and signed the crushed windshield, which eventually wound up on display at the Chicago Sports Museum at Water Tower Place.

But this is an excellent lesson. Don't park your car near Field 1 in Mesa!

Or, as I learned on another visit to the practice fields, don't park your pickup truck in the first spot across from Field 5. Another batting-practice ball flew over a 25-foot-high screen and at least 25 feet farther and dented the pickup's door. My car was only four spots over from this. I'm not sure who hit that baseball, but lesson learned: park farther away and get some exercise by walking up to the fields in Mesa when the Cubs are hitting.

I attended a couple more of these drills, and then it was on to the first practice game of 2016.

***

"Maryvale" sounds like a subdivision name created by a "Mad Men"-era PR guy to try to entice people to move somewhere they wouldn't otherwise have gone, to create a pleasant suburban feel to a gritty city neighborhood.

That is, in fact, exactly what it was. Maryvale, not an actual suburb but part of the city of Phoenix, was an area being converted from industry to residence in the 1950s and, for a time, provided inexpensive tract homes for middle-income residents. By the 1980s and 1990s, the area was in decline, and urban planners looked for ways to revitalize the area. This dovetailed nicely with then-Arizona Gov. Rose Mofford's desire to keep major-league clubs in the Phoenix area for spring training and to attract new teams.

And that is how Maryvale Baseball Park got built, opening in 1998, enticing the Brewers to move there from Chandler, Arizona. The city and state hoped that the complex would help bring new development into the area.

It never happened. Maryvale's still a dodgy area, and despite the fact that the ballpark has lights, the Brewers don't play any nighttime spring games there. It's a fine venue to watch a ballgame, but not to linger after, as many do after attending games at spring parks in Scottsdale and Mesa.

I wouldn't normally go to a Cubs game there—been there, done that—but the 2016 schedule had the Cubs playing their first spring game at Maryvale, and it felt right to begin the season's journey with the very first contest.

Maryvale Baseball Park is like retro spring training in many ways. The park has no video board and a PA announcer who sounds like they've had to brush the cobwebs off him before he opens the mic. In announcing the lineups, he called the Cubs' first baseman Anthony "REET-zo," which would be correct if we were in Italy, but it doesn't really sound right for spring ball in Arizona. Thus, Maryvale is kind of a gentle trip into spring training the way it used to be, where the places were half-full and no one really cared much about what was going on down on the field.

Only 4,279 somewhat-interested folks paid to see this game on March 3, 2016, which was by far the smallest crowd to see the Cubs all spring. Of the Cubs' 15 home games at Sloan Park, all but one (March 7 vs. the Royals, a game added after the schedule had already been announced) sold out, and even most of the Cubs' away games drew well over 10,000, with most of the other teams recording their biggest crowd of the spring when the Cubs were the visitors.

The baseball story of that first day was Javier Baez, whom the Cubs were trying out in center field to see if he could use his defensive versatility in the outfield. That day for Javy can charitably be called an "adventure."

The very first play of the Brewers' first inning was a ball hit over his head onto the tall hitters' background. Javy let the ball play him. Result: triple.

When managers make these kinds of player placements, it often seems that makes them baseball magnets. The second hitter of the game also hit the ball in Javy's direction. He caught it, made a bit of a wild throw somewhere in the direction of the plate, 1–0 Brewers. Milwaukee catcher Jonathan Lucroy was the next batter. He also hit a ball to Baez. Or, rather, in the general area of right-center field. Jorge Soler headed in that direction, but Javy called him off the ball . . . and dropped it for a two-base error.

The Cubs eventually lost the game, 2–1, with the only run driven in by Dan Vogelbach, who wasn't expected to make the team (and didn't). March had begun hot, as February 2016 had been in the Phoenix area, and the 90-degree high (16 degrees above the average high for the date) made the whole thing feel more summer-like than spring training normally does.

And this wound up being a curious thing: Despite all the brave talk of Javy being a backup center fielder during the season, the number of innings he played there during the 2016 campaign was zero. (He played only one batter's worth of time anywhere in the outfield all year, during an extra-inning win over the Brewers at Miller Park on May 18.)

The next afternoon, Friday, March 4, the Cubs opened their Sloan Park home spring season against the Los Angeles Angels, and just a few more people showed up.

All right, a lot more people showed up. The crowd of 15,446 set a new Cactus League record, and the Cubs got solid pitching from eight different pitchers, only two of whom would actually pitch in the big leagues for the team in 2016. They shut out the Angels, 3–0, got a home run from Addison Russell and some solid defense from "Grandpa" David Ross, so nicknamed by Anthony Rizzo and Kris Bryant, who created an Instagram account in honor of the oldest player on the team to chronicle Ross's final year in a big-league uniform. This is just one example of the camaraderie and closeness of the 2016 Cubs. It's impossible to measure the effects of clubhouse chemistry on a team winning—obviously, better talent beats lesser talent most of the time—but I firmly believe things like this do matter.

The Cubs, who were still tweaking Sloan Park in its third season, installed a ribbon board on the first-base facade, a welcome addition for fans sitting on the left-field berm (like me!) or down the third-base line, who couldn't see the video board, which is set back from the field on top of the left-field party deck.

So the Cubs evened up their spring record at 1–1 and then promptly lost seven games in a row. Which means exactly nothing. This is because spring training, for players, has become a place where the expected 25-man roster players enter games for a few innings, get their work in, and then are replaced by guys from the minor-league camp. It's different if the team involved has positional battles or rotation slots that need to be filled, but this was not the case for the 2016 Cubs. Various nonroster players who got invitations to 2016 Cubs spring training such as Juan Perez, Jean Machi, and Shane Victorino—all of whom had previously played in World Series—had little chance of making the 25-man roster. So it was more interesting to watch guys like Munenori Kawasaki, who performed karaoke for his teammates during some pregame practices, try to make the squad, or at least entertain fans.

Other than that, the spring contests are tune-ups for the starting rotation, which results in some disappointment among fans when someone like Jake Arrieta starts a game and departs after three innings. There's an informal agreement, pushed by Major League Baseball, that all teams should bring at least four "regulars," or at least guys who will make the big-league squad, to away games. In practice, this doesn't always happen, which in some ways isn't fair to people who are paying what now come close to big-league prices for practice games. The Giants, for example, charged as much as $40 for lawn tickets for certain spring games, which is quite expensive for what amounts to glorified Double-A baseball.

This produces a dichotomy in the types of fans who attend spring-training games. Sloan Park has the largest capacity of any park in the Cactus League, 15,200 (though that number was breached in 14 of the 15 home games), and since there is a large number of expatriate Chicagoans living in the Phoenix area, many of these people crowd into spring games, since it's among the only times they can see their heroes in person. Many of these people cheer exuberantly, desperately exhorting the Cubs to win, even though by the late innings, most of those "Cubs" are players who will spend the summer in Myrtle Beach or South Bend, not Chicago.

Then there are the fans who can spend a weekend, or a week, in the Valley of the Sun and many times are more interested in having a few beers with their friends, or getting a tan (most often, this turns into an angry pink sunburn, as people don't heed warnings that sunscreen is a must), than the result of the game.

That's one reason the prices have spiraled somewhat out of control. I spoke to one pair of Giants fans who were standing behind me in line for the game between their team and the Cubs at Sloan Park on March 26. They'd bought tickets via StubHub, in section 119, nice box seats down the first-base line, which have a face value of $38 each. How much did they pay? $100 each.

I suppose that this is just supply and demand; no one forced those folks to fork over a C-note to see a game where big-league players mostly depart by the fifth inning. But this shows you just how much spring training has changed. Thirty-two years ago, I walked into Phoenix Municipal Stadium for my very first spring game between the Cubs and Athletics. I bought a box seat for $3.

This isn't a "get off my lawn" complaint. I certainly don't expect pricing for spring training, or anything, to be the same as it was three decades ago, and the dream of a $3 spring ticket died with the turn of the millennium. But one of the best things about spring training was the laid-back atmosphere at games and the ability to see big-league entertainment for $10 or less.

It's all become a profit center now, big business, and I suppose you can't blame the teams for seeing the dollar signs. But in doing so, the previous feeling of spring training as a pleasant diversion to while away a few hours watching baseball in March sunshine has in many ways been lost, and I'm not sure we're better off for it.

The year 2016 was my 27th spring training, and in going to as many games as I have, I've met many people from all walks of life and places around the country, and fallen in with a group of regulars who enjoy the left-field lawn. We occupied a spot in front of the old scoreboard at HoHoKam Park when the Cubs trained there and moved to a similar spot near the left-field line at Sloan Park. Most of these folks, many originally from the Chicago area or the Midwest, take these games as opportunities to socialize with friends. It winds up being a party more than anyone taking a baseball game seriously, and who could blame them? The score really doesn't matter, only that you are enjoying perfect 80-degree sunshine with your best baseball buds. (And when I say "buds," that can also refer to the beer that gets consumed in copious amounts, both in pregame tailgates and on the lawn.)

Ron, George, Ken, Miriam, and I generally get to Sloan Park early, along with a few other friends and some who come in and out of town as the month goes on, as we enjoy being the first people in the park, and to socialize before the game.

I take these games a bit more seriously while also socializing. I keep score at all the spring games I attend, just as I do at Wrigley Field and other parks I travel to during the regular season. It's not often easy, with multiple substitutions coming early on in games, and many of the players not even listed on the expanded 65-man spring roster. I consider it spring training for scorekeeping. You might ask, "Why keep score when you can look up all these numbers on your phone?" Part of it is keeping a baseball routine I've maintained for decades, something I've always done and that just feels like part of the game to me. What it really is, though, is about history. Sure, you can find box scores and stats anywhere online these days. Writing down those numbers as they happen, though, personalizes the history for you. It makes me feel part of the game, to a very small extent, and I keep all the cards, sometimes referring to them years later—again, even though all these numbers are online via baseball-reference.com and retrosheet.org, both websites invaluable to any baseball researcher or fan. Some of Retrosheet's numbers are actually mine, in fact—I sent them about 90 scorecard scans a number of years ago when they were collecting play-by-play of games they did not then have in their database, all now a part of the fabric of baseball history.

Further, I like to keep up with what Joe Maddon's doing with his rostered and nonrostered players and guys dragged over from the minor-league camp. Joe and his coaching staff don't sit in the dugout, either, during spring games. They'll sit on folding chairs in front of the front-row seats next to the dugout, likely so they can discuss what's going on with the players without any of them eavesdropping. This isn't just a Cubs thing, either; pretty much all the coaching staffs do this for spring games.

Finally, after seven straight defeats, the Cubs at last won another game, before yet another sellout crowd at Sloan Park on Friday, March 11. The 7–4 win over the Reds featured home runs from guys who wouldn't make the team (Dan Vogelbach and Tim

Federowicz) and three innings' worth of work from John Lackey, who was making his first start . . . not in Cubs home pinstripes, as the team had always worn during spring games, but in the spring blue top now mandated by Major League Baseball. MLB's marketing folks had decided that Spring Training (now capitalized) should be a "jewel event," as the All-Star Game and Postseason (what a Capital idea!) are, and thus each team was asked to create a special, colored jersey just for spring games. In the Cubs' case this shirt was nearly identical to the blue alternate jersey the team wears occasionally for regular-season road games. To me, something special about spring training was lost here because the Cubs had been just about the last team to wear their usual home whites at their spring park. Now, they'd have to be just like everyone else under an MLB mandate, another not-so-good sign of the corporatizing of baseball.

The Cubs play "Go Cubs Go" at Sloan Park after wins, just as they do at Wrigley Field, but somehow singing this for a game where the guys high-fiving after the win included Taylor Davis, John Andreoli, Bryant Flete, and Jason Vosler didn't quite seem right.

Two days later, the Cubs made their annual pilgrimage to their former home park, now renamed HoHoKam Stadium. It's been refurbished in green and gold as the spring home of the Oakland Athletics. The city of Mesa did a nice job redoing the park that was the Cubs' spring home from 1997–2013 (and a previous version of that park, with the same name, stood on the same site from 1979–96); they removed a section of bleachers down the left-field line and replaced it with a party deck, reducing the capacity to about 10,000. That alone shows you the difference in popularity between the Cubs, who routinely sold out the old 13,000 capacity, and the A's, who needed the presence of several thousand Cubs fans for the sellout of 10,040 on this sunny Sunday, one of just three sellouts the A's had this spring.

This was the second time my left-field lawn compatriots and I had returned to HoHoKam since it reopened in 2015 as Oakland's spring home, and being in our former spot on the berm felt familiar, yet strange. Even with many Cubs fans in attendance, the crowd felt more California laid-back, and the game went swiftly, with Kyle Hendricks throwing four strong innings (the first Cubs starter to go four in camp) and Travis Wood and Pedro Strop also providing strong relief. The Cubs entered the ninth inning with a 3–0 lead.

Hector Rondon, making his second spring appearance, wasn't good. After a sharp line drive to second produced the first out, three seeing-eye singles sandwiched around a walk produced two runs, and a sacrifice fly tied the game. While Rondon's fastball had decent velocity, it had little movement, and the A's capitalized. Hector got out of the inning, and that's when a curious thing that only happens in spring training, happened.

The game ended in a 3–3 tie. Yes, there are still ties in spring baseball, even though they've been eliminated from regular-season games. Since teams are generally just trying to get work in for their regular players and pitchers, once that's done, the game is declared done, even if it's tied. The Cubs had played two games the day before, split-squad contests against the White Sox and Dodgers, and thus only brought enough pitchers to HoHoKam for nine innings. Generally, in modern spring training, teams won't play more than 10-inning games, by mutual agreement, and this one was mutually agreed to end after nine. It's also a courtesy to the visiting team. In the Cactus League, teams usually dress at their home park, take batting practice there if they choose, and then bus to the away site. Some players even drive their own cars, in uniform, which makes for occasional odd sightings on area freeways (yes, that probably was a Cubs player, driving his expensive sports car, right next to you on the Loop 101!).

The Cubs played a pair of tie games in spring 2016. Some teams played as many as five. In some ways, this isn't fair to the paying customer, who'd like to see some kind of resolution to the contest, but I certainly understand the team's need to protect players from injury in games that don't mean anything.

One thing that happened to me during spring training 2016 dated back to the Cubs' postseason run in October 2015. Around the time I was racing from Chicago to Pittsburgh to St. Louis and back to Chicago, I did something to my neck. It might have been from opening a car door the wrong way or picking up a piece of luggage that was too heavy. I didn't notice anything at the time, but a few weeks later, around the time the Cubs were quietly exiting the postseason at the hands of the Mets, I began to have some pain in my right arm, right above my elbow. At the time, I had no idea where that had come from, but the pain made it difficult at times to write my stories for Bleed Cubbie Blue, and eventually it got bad enough that it began waking me up in the middle of the night.

I got misdiagnosed by one doctor; another gave me a prescription that made the pain go away for a while, but in January it came back and at times was excruciating.

A number of years ago, I had seen a chiropractor in Chicago, who did good work on me, and I never did find another one I liked after she moved to California. So with no help from medical doctors on this issue, I thought I'd try that again and fired up the Google machine to find one near where I stay in the Phoenix area.

By chance, I happened to find a chiropractor who treats major-league baseball players as part of her practice. (There's lots of signed memorabilia in her office, too.)

I saw Dr. Alicia Myers several times just before spring-training games began, and through a combination of massage and chiropractic adjustment, the pain in my arm was gone. As it turned out, I had a pinched nerve in my neck that was radiating pain down my right arm. If you've had one of those, you know how extremely painful they can be. I'm really lucky to have found someone who's really good at what she does.

I asked Dr. Myers to give me an idea of what she does to help ballplayers, of course without revealing any personal information (she can't, due to HIPAA laws):

When a player first comes in, it is usually because their trainer has tried everything possible in the clubhouse to fix them but there's an issue with either pain, loss of motion, chronic usage, tendonitis, or overall well-being that still needs to be addressed. Many of the players have told me that I do a very extensive one-hour exam. After this orthopedic, neurological, and chiropractic exam, I determine if radiographs are needed. If so, we take all needed X-rays, and I have the player come back the next day or later after I have had time to sit down and study all the results.

When I have determined the cause of the problem, the magic begins to happen! I want to make sure that all of their nerves are functioning at 100 percent capacity. Seth Sharpless, a professor of neuroscience at the University of Colorado, did a study that found that the pressure/weight of one quarter against a nerve can decreases its nerve conduction velocity by 60 percent. Think about this . . . this means that baseball players affected by this might only be able to use 40 percent of their full capacity when playing a game! Thus, if I do a gentle diversified adjustment to the bone that is putting pressure on the nerve, and relieve that pressure that can increase the range of motion in the shoulder. In the case of pitchers, it can help them regain lost velocity.

To verify this, I always have my player lie on their back on my table. I then have him lift his arm up and "hold it" while I try to push it down. If there is a pinched nerve somewhere I (and I'm a woman weighing only a buck 50) can easily push their arm down with little pressure. The areas that usually present issues are neck, mid-back, the acromioclavicular joint (the joint at the top of the shoulder), or even the sternoclavicular joint (the joint between the sternum and clavicle). Each player is different in his core strength and mobility, but usually it only takes about five minutes to repair the neurological issue, and the player is then retested. If the correction is complete, his arm strength can improve by as much as 60 percent, and it is very noticeable. Usually the player is amazed at the difference he experiences.

Chiropractic is used in sports not only to help those in pain, but also to function better overall.

Chiropractic isn't for everyone, but I can tell you it worked wonders for me, and Dr. Myers says she's helped many baseball players who are suffering nerve issues return to full functioning.

Spring games carried on. ESPN, aware that the Cubs were becoming a story even before the season began, asked for two of their games for Thursday evening preseason specials. This sounds great, but it makes for an odd game-going experience. Most spring games are played during the day, as that's when most vacation-goers and many locals want to see them, as they often have other plans in the evening, and also, the lighting plants at spring parks aren't really big-league quality; they're more like those you'd see at a Double-A or Triple-A ballpark.

So most teams play one or two night games per spring. These ESPN games, though . . . Eastern time zone bias won out for them, and as Arizona doesn't observe Daylight Saving Time and is three hours behind Eastern time, the games were moved to 4 p.m. Arizona time (or 7 p.m. ET). This means shadows on the field and cool conditions once the sun sets around 6:30.

On the other hand, it's not so bad when you don't have to fight rush-hour traffic after a 1:05 p.m contest that lets out just when Loop 101 is starting to back up.

One event I always look forward to is the Cubs' wives annual charity garage sale, which this year happened Friday, March 25, before a game against the Brewers. Usually, there are just jerseys and other team-issued memorabilia as well as "mystery balls," where you buy a baseball in a bag not knowing who signed it, but this year the famed Kyle Schwarber Windshield was being auctioned to help benefit Cubs Charities. That raised $900, and I helped out Cubs Charities by being among the first to look through the selection of team-issued jerseys. A Pedro Strop game-worn shirt was on the top of the pile. It had the "AZ 2016" patch on the sleeve, a nice souvenir of the spring for $85. Another $20 for a coach's pullover (similar to the one you see pitching coach Chris Bosio wear when he makes mound visits) made this a good "shopping" trip to get team gear at reasonable prices, as well as help out Cubs Charities.

There was one more notable event as players and fans entered the final week of tune-up games. Spring break for most schools is over by then, and even though the games were still sold out, the lawn at Sloan Park felt a bit less crowded Wednesday, March 30, when the Cubs took on the Rockies. Jon Lester took the mound for his final spring tune-up before the regular season opener.

In the fourth inning, with the Cubs already leading 3–0, Lester came to the plate.

You might guess something notable happened here, and you'd be right. The backstory, though, is that Jon Lester is one of the worst-hitting pitchers in major-league history, and that is no exaggeration. (Though he is a pretty good bunter; he once put down three successful sacrifices in 2015 game, just the fifth time any Cubs pitcher had ever done that, and one of the other four was Greg Maddux.) Lester set an all-time record for the most at-bats before his first major-league hit, 66, and the single that broke this mark was off his friend and now-teammate John Lackey. Even after that, going into the 2016 season, Lester was 4-for-98 in his career (.041), all singles, with 52 strikeouts.

On this pleasant March afternoon in Mesa, though, Lester turned into a power hitter. He lofted a 3–1 pitch from Scott Oberg—a guy with actual big-league experience who was in the Rockies bullpen for much of 2015 and 2016, not a minor-leaguer—onto the left-field berm for a two-run homer. It landed about 50 feet from me, and unless all 15,108 of us in attendance that afternoon were under a mass hallucination, it really happened.

To the opposite field, no less. Lester later told reporters it was his first homer "since high school."

And to date, his last, and since it was in a spring game, it won't show up in the record books. Lester didn't really hit any better in the 2016 season, though he did collect his first two career extra-base hits (both doubles) and walked five times, and he led the team in sacrifice bunts.

The Cubs wound up winning that game against the Rockies, 10–0, not that spring wins and losses matter at all. They went 11–19—the second-worst record in the Cactus League. Only the Padres (10–21) were worse.

With the spring season over, Miriam and I began to pack up to drive back to Chicago. This would be a much easier task in 2016 than it was in 2015, when the spring schedule ended Thursday, April 2, and ESPN asked for the Cubs/Cardinals season opener to be moved up to Sunday, April 5. That necessitated driving from Phoenix to Chicago on Friday and Saturday and being at the ballpark Sunday, which would be a tiring schedule for professional athletes, never mind two fans. We were exhausted for a month.

When the Cubs' 2016 schedule noted the home opener would be Monday, April 11, I breathed a sigh of relief. We decided to stick in Arizona to watch the season-opening two-game set against the Angels in Anaheim on TV (and it's much more pleasant to watch West Coast games on TV when they don't end at midnight where you are) April 4 and 5, then drive back to Chicago April 6 and 7 and be back home in time to catch the series opener against the Diamondbacks in Phoenix the evening of April 7. (If only the MLB schedulers had flip-flopped those two, we'd have stayed to see them play the D-backs.)

The plan worked; the 25-hour drive that covers about 1,700 miles landed us at home in Chicago only a few minutes after the first pitch had been thrown in Phoenix between the Cubs and D-backs.

And that was just the beginning of the best Cubs regular season in my lifetime.

Chapter 4

April: Roaring Ahead of Everyone

A naheim, California. (Not Azusa, not Cucamonga.)
That's not a traditional season-opening spot for the Chicago Cubs; usually, the regular season begins in the home of one of the team's NL Central rivals (St. Louis, Pittsburgh, Milwaukee, or Cincinnati), or at Wrigley Field.

The 2016 season, though, not only would open on the West Coast, but for the first time, the Cubs would play an American League team in its first two regular-season games. Year-round interleague play was made necessary when the Astros moved to the American League in 2013, giving each league an odd number of teams (15).

So the Cubs would begin the year using the designated hitter, and there had never been any doubt as to who the starting pitcher designated for Opening Day would be.

Jake Arrieta, owner of the 2015 Cy Young Award and a half-season that year that was better than anyone's since the Deadball Era, got the call. Jake had suffered from a blister that forced him out of a spring game against the Giants a couple of weeks prior, but in this game, he had that 2015 dominance working for him. Seven shutout innings, two singles, and a walk made his 89-pitch outing seem almost effortless.

Miguel Montero, who'd had an excellent spring, homered and drove in three runs; Dexter Fowler added three hits and scored three runs, and the Cubs crushed the Angels, 9–0.

The next night, it was Jon Lester's turn, and he nearly matched his teammate's performance, allowing just a single run in a 6–1 win.

And it wasn't too early to start thinking like this: it might not seem like such a big deal, taking a two-game set from a team that has some issues, but (here's a statistic that might, or might not, mean something) it had been 21 years since any Cubs team won its first two games. In the labor stoppage-shortened 1995 season of 144 games, the Cubs went 2–0 by taking a series in Cincinnati. That year didn't wind up a playoff season, but the 1995 Cubs did finish with a winning record, 73–71.

In fact, Cubs teams haven't done this sort of thing very often at all. Here are all the years from 1900 through 2015 where the Cubs began 2–0:

> 1902, 1906, 1907, 1908, 1917, 1921, 1922, 1931, 1934, 1938, 1946, 1950, 1951, 1955, 1958, 1969, 1973, 1974, 1984, 1984, 1995

In reality, there's only one thing any team should think after 2–0, and that is: you have 160 more games to go. That list is a strange mix of pennant-winning and playoff years, contending years, and bad seasons. But only 21 times in 116 years? You'd think there would have been more.

The Cubs then took their 2–0 record back to the desert, to begin a four-game series against the Diamondbacks at Chase Field.

And not long after I walked into my house after the drive back from Arizona, I saw something on my TV that brought thoughts of "Oh, no!" to the 2016 season.

In the bottom of the second inning of the first game of the series against the D-backs, with the Cubs trailing 3–2 and two out, Jean Segura lofted a fly ball to deep left-center field. Kyle Schwarber and Dexter Fowler both ran after the ball.

Even after looking at the video of this play way too many times, I still can't figure out how Schwarber got hurt, but the collision between Fowler and Schwarber left Kyle with a torn ACL and LCL, an injury so serious, he was almost immediately ruled out for the season. Fowler, fortunately, was OK; Segura wound up rounding the bases for an inside-the-park home run.

Despite that, and John Lackey's shaky first Cub start (six runs in six innings), the Cubs won the game, 14–6. Anthony Rizzo had three hits, including a home run, and drove in six. I suspect the Cubs would have traded that win for Schwarber's health.

Theo Epstein & Co. had spent several seasons trying to produce enough depth in the system, through drafting, trades, and free agency, to weather an injury like this one. Now, just three games into 2016, this depth was going to be tested. Could the Cubs win without Schwarber's power bat?

Instead of going into the system for an outfielder to replace Schwarber, the Cubs recalled infielder Munenori Kawasaki, who was known more for his cut-up humor around the clubhouse than for his on-field performance, and the Cubs would fill in the left-field hole by giving more playing time to Jorge Soler and Matt Szczur, as well as some outfield time for Ben Zobrist and Kris Bryant, as Mad Scientist Joe Maddon plugged in players all over the field.

The team's first game sans Schwarber wound up as a tough loss. Behind solid starting pitching from Jason Hammel, they took a 2–1 lead into the bottom of the eighth, but the D-backs got a two-out RBI single in that inning off Pedro Strop to tie it, and in the ninth, a two-out RBI single off Trevor Cahill gave Arizona the win.

The Cubs dropped to 3–1, and out of first place by a game, as the Pirates were off to a 4–0 start. Shows you how much that means. That was the only day all season the Cubs were not in first place, and the Pirates wound up under .500 at 78–83.

They moved back into first place with a Saturday win over the D-backs, and Sunday produced a series win behind Jake Arrieta, who not only continued his pitching dominance, but hit a colossal 442-foot home run to center field, the seventh-longest homer slugged by any Cubs hitter in 2016.

With a successful 5–1 season-opening road trip, the Cubs headed to Chicago for the Wrigley Field opener, the second consecutive year they'd opened at home with a night game.

Some fans complained about this. The 2015 evening season debut had been acceptable, as it was ESPN's choice for their Sunday night season opener. But many didn't care for a Monday Opening Night.

There was a logical reason for the choice. Since the Cubs were playing a Sunday afternoon game in Arizona, which operates two hours behind Chicago during the baseball season, that game ended after 6 p.m. Chicago time. With a three-hour flight and the two-hour time difference, it meant an arrival in Chicago after midnight Monday. Playing an afternoon game wouldn't have been fair to Cubs players. Other fans noted the off-day Tuesday and asked why the Cubs wouldn't have opened then, taking Monday off.

There was a logical reason for that, too. Teams in cold-weather cities often have off days after their home openers, in case the scheduled opener gets rained out. That way they can have a second chance at an "Opening Day" celebration if there's a postponement, rather than just have the second scheduled game be the opener.

Fans might have grumbled, but 40,882 crowded Wrigley Field for the April 11 home opener against the Reds. Before the game, and not long after their late-night arrival from Phoenix, the Cubs got a tour of their spectacular new 30,000 square-foot clubhouse (now second-biggest in baseball, behind only the Yankees), which had been constructed over the offseason. The new clubhouse includes a huge locker room, a strength and conditioning center, training areas, offices, a media center and interview room, and an expansive players-only lounge. The training facilities became immediately important; the rehab center allowed Kyle Schwarber to spend much of the season with his teammates. If the injury had happened a year earlier, he would have had to rehab at the Cubs' spring complex in Mesa. Instead, Schwarber, who spent most home games in the dugout, could feel part of the team even though he played just two regular-season games in 2016.

I was fortunate enough to be included on a media tour of the clubhouse. It is as spectacular as you've heard. The Cubs even included a memorabilia display that's visible from the workout room. Cubs President of Business Operations Crane Kenney told me that they wanted Cubs players to understand the rich history of the franchise and what they were part of, while they were working out. They spared no expense, and I don't think it's a coincidence that the clubhouse opened the same year this marvelous season took place. With players having top-notch facilities, it was easy for them to have top-notch performance. They also created a "party room," complete with a fog machine, speakers for party music, and a lighted, spinning disco ball, in an area that had been the players' lounge in the old clubhouse (with the rest of that area turned into batting cages). The plan for the "party room" was to have players go in there to celebrate wins, let off steam for a few minutes, then go back into the new digs and begin preparation for the next game. It worked well, 57 times during the 2016 regular season, even though after one August win the fog machine apparently worked a bit too well, setting off the Wrigley fire alarms.

That started on the very first day of home games at Wrigley Field. In addition to the clubhouse, the team spent the winter continuing the renovations to the ballpark. They replaced a large number of seats on the left-field side and also completed the new bleacher structure, which had been about 70 percent finished for 2015. Among things added to the bleachers were memorabilia and history displays for fans. My friend Mike was among those asked to contribute to these displays, and I saw people pause and look at them virtually every day. It was an excellent way of connecting the new ballpark structure to the team's past. They also installed an ersatz ivy wall underneath the right-field bleachers for photo ops, and paintings of Cubs Hall of Famers, along with replicas of their Cooperstown plaques.

The bleachers certainly aren't the "cheap seats," as they were for decades, anymore. But the amenities the Cubs have added to the new, expanded bleacher structure have certainly made the experience better.

And then it was time for baseball, on a chilly, 48-degree evening—but not before the Cubs asked fans to show up earlier than usual and opened half an hour before they normally would (4:35 p.m for a 7:05 p.m. start) because they were operating Wrigley for the first time with MLB-mandated magnetometer checks. The lines moved steadily, and for a shakedown cruise, the checks worked reasonably well, though the Cubs would tweak the procedure several times during the season.

The traditional player introductions featured one thing that brought a huge ovation, larger than you'd usually hear on Opening Day: Kyle Schwarber walking slowly to the line of players, in full uniform, on crutches, an emotional time for everyone in the park. Then, at last, it was time for baseball.

Even with Jon Lester throwing reasonably well, the Cubs trailed, 3–0, going into the bottom of the seventh, as Brandon Finnegan took a no-hitter into that inning. David Ross, of all people, broke it up with a single, and after Finnegan walked pinch-hitter Matt Szczur, the Reds went to their bullpen.

It wasn't known at the time how bad the Cincinnati bullpen would be in 2016, but in this game they began what turned into a major-league record streak, 23 straight games in which Reds relievers allowed at least one run. Caleb Cotham allowed a two-run single to Jason Heyward, the runs charged to Finnegan, making it 3–2. In the next inning, Ben Zobrist walked and Jorge Soler was hit by a pitch. Jumbo Diaz, one of my favorite baseball names, entered to pitch for the Reds, and Addison Russell sent his first pitch into the bleachers to give the Cubs a 5–3 lead, "as the crowd went wild."

The Ross and Heyward singles and the Russell homer were the Cubs' only hits of the game, making it just the fourth time in franchise history (and first since 1969) that the Cubs had won a game scoring five runs on only three hits.

This wouldn't be the last time we'd begin hearing comparisons of the 2016 team to great Cubs teams of the past.

The Cubs continued their dominance over the Reds. They posted five-run innings in each of the subsequent two games of the three-game Wrigley set, in the first inning April 13 and the eighth inning April 14, on their way to a sweep. Kris Bryant homered in both games, and the Cubs drew a total of 15 walks off the Reds' beleaguered pitching staff, which led to the beginning of keeping a "walk watch." The 1975 Cubs had set the team record for walks in a season, 650. Four decades' worth of impatience at the plate had kept that record intact (though it was nearly broken by the 2008 team, which had 638 walks). This year's Cubs finally broke that mark with 656 bases on balls.

The wins also gave the Cubs a five-game winning streak and an 8–1 record and a three-game lead in the division. With just nine games played.

And then the Colorado Rockies came to Wrigley Field.

The teams split the first two games, and then the Cubs had to face Tyler Chatwood, who was expected to be one of the Rox's best pitchers in 2016.

He did not disappoint, at least not for Rockies fans. His defense made several good plays behind him, a blast by Jon Lester (of all people) was held in by a Lake Michigan breeze for a double instead of a home run, and the Cubs, though they had the tying runs on base in the ninth inning, lost 2–0. Even though it was still mid-April, there was a definite playoff-type atmosphere at Wrigley Field in the bottom of the ninth. Almost no one left early, and the crowd was on its feet cheering and yelling for a rally— something we haven't seen in years, if ever, in April. And this was just the sixth home game of 2016.

So the Cubs lost their first series of the year to a team that wasn't expected to be in contention, and the one game they won created a weird little footnote, if you are into name wordplay.

In the Cubs' 6–2 win over the Rockies Saturday, April 16, Matt Szczur got the start against Colorado's Christian Bergmann to give

Jason Heyward a breather. Having a fourth outfielder get an occasional start is not usually something you'd read about in a book, but hear me out.

Bergmann departed for a pinch-hitter in the sixth inning, and Rockies manager Walt Weiss sent right-handed reliever David Hale into the game. Hale threw a scoreless sixth, and with the Cubs leading, 2–0, he went out to begin the seventh. Addison Russell tried to bunt his way on and was thrown out, and that brought up Szczur.

Well, come on. Say it out loud. You should know by now the Cubs outfielder's last name is pronounced the same as the ancient Roman emperor Caesar. And so this was the first-ever "Hale/Szczur" matchup.

No columns crumbled nor was anyone there to say "Et tu?" but Szczur won the battle, singling off Hale. Then he stole second. After David Ross walked, Dexter Fowler hit a three-run homer that pretty much sealed the win.

So hail Szczur for that one, anyway.

After the Rockies series, the Cubs headed to St. Louis and Cincinnati for their first road trip into the parks of their NL Central rivals.

John Lackey showed his old mates what they were missing, throwing seven shutout innings with 11 strikeouts in a 5–0 Cubs win in the series opener, and the Cubs took two of three. And I'm glossing over the series against the Cardinals, because what happened in Cincinnati was far more significant.

When the Cubs were no-hit by Cole Hamels on July 25, 2015, it broke a streak of 7,920 consecutive games in which the Cubs had at least one hit, going back nearly 50 years to Sandy Koufax's perfect game against them September 9, 1965. That's the all-time major-league record for such things, and though it didn't get the Cubs anything but that recognition, it was still kind of neat to have, made more fun by the @CubsNoHitStreak Twitter account, which duly recognized every first hit of a game and tweeted out other fun facts about "The Streak," as it was dubbed, and the Cubs.

The no-hitter put the Cubs back at the bottom of the "Last Time They Were No Hit" list, and the Reds, who had not been no-hit during the regular season (Roy Halladay of Philadelphia no-hit them during the 2010 NL Division Series) since Rick Wise of the Phillies did it June 23, 1971, moved to the top of the list. Entering the game on April 21 in Cincinnati, the Reds' no-hit streak had reached 7,109 games, oddly enough, exactly one game more than five years away from matching the Cubs' record stretch.

I had jokingly said to some of my friends late in 2015, after Jake Arrieta had no-hit the Dodgers, that I wanted his next no-hitter to be against the Reds, in order to break their streak.

And darned if he didn't do just that, on Thursday, April 21, in front of an announced crowd of 16,497 at Great American Ballpark in Cincinnati. He wasn't quite as dominant as in his first no-no, as he issued four walks. The outcome of the game was really never in doubt, as the Cubs plated a pair of runs in each of the first two innings and led, 9–0, by the sixth. And as great as Jake's no-hitter was, it was nearly overshadowed by Kris Bryant's big night. The Cubs third baseman went 4-for-6, scored four runs and drove in six, and the Cubs poured seven runs on the beleaguered Reds bullpen in the last three innings to win, 16–0. Some other fun facts about Jake's second career no-hitter:

- It was Jake's second no-hitter in his *last 11 regular-season* starts dating back to the August 2015 no-no against the Dodgers.
- It was the most runs scored by a winning team in a no-hitter since the pitching distance was moved to 60 feet, six inches in 1893. The only no-hitter in which there were more runs scored was on August 4, 1884, when future Hall of Famer Pud Galvin of the Buffalo Bisons beat the Detroit Wolverines, 18–0. Since 1900, the previous record for most runs by the winner in a no-hitter had been 15, on September 6, 1905, when Frank Smith of the White Sox no-hit the Tigers, 15–0.
- It reduced Jake's season ERA to 0.87.

- Even with four walks—twice as many as he'd allowed all year to date—Jake's WHIP dropped to 0.677.
- The Cubs had outscored the Reds, 38–6, in the four games the teams played to that date, winning all of them.

And for those of us who are aficionados of curiosities like no-hit streaks, the Oakland Athletics took over the top spot on the "longest without a no-hitter against them" streak. The A's were last no-hit July 14, 1991, so their streak stood at 4,059 games through the end of the 2016 season, meaning they were a little less than 24 years away from breaking the Cubs' record streak entering 2017.

I think the Cubs' record is pretty safe.

The Cubs took three of four in Cincinnati and stood at 13–5 overall, coming back to Wrigley to play a scheduled six-game homestand against the Brewers and Braves.

I say "scheduled" because only four of the six games on the homestand were played. The Cubs had a day off Monday, April 25, and on the 26th hosted the Brewers on a night not fit for baseball. It was 40 degrees at game time with a wind howling in off the lake at 16 miles per hour, and I felt that night's chill again just typing those words.

The Cubs trailed 1–0 in the fifth when Joe Maddon pinch-hit for starter Kyle Hendricks, an unusual strategy that early in the game, but Joe usually knows best. Tommy La Stella batted and walked to load the bases. Dexter Fowler hit a ball that might have been a grand slam if not for the wind; the sacrifice fly tied the game, so Joe's move did pay off.

A more important play happened in the seventh, as Javier Baez was called out trying to steal second with the Cubs leading, 3–1. Javy immediately signaled to the dugout to have the replay crew take a look—and he was right. He'd pulled his left hand out of the way of Jonathan Villar's tag while keeping his right hand on the base, a nice heads-up move. He later scored on a double by Anthony Rizzo. This was the first play overturned on replay challenge at Wrigley in 2016, and Baez's run turned out to be the game-winner in a 4–3 Cubs victory.

The next day's weather forecast wasn't much better, but the Cubs dutifully opened the gates to Wrigley Field at the usual time, 5 p.m., for a night game. A little more than an hour later, they sent out a press release that postponed the game due to "the forecast for inclement weather throughout the remainder of the evening."

This weather forecast was known . . . as I noted, the previous day. Rain was expected to begin by early afternoon and continue all evening. As it turned out, it didn't start to rain in the area around Wrigley until about 3:30, but once it started, it didn't stop.

The Cubs did the right thing by calling off this game . . . but they could have heeded the forecast and called the game before the gates even opened. I'd say there were no more than maybe 2,000 or so people in the park when the game was called, so I can't imagine food sales were too brisk, although I did have something to eat myself before hearing the game-called announcement and heading home.

I'm glad that game was postponed. It would have been risky to wait, then send Jake Arrieta out to start and then potentially have the game delayed, in which case his outing could have been wasted. It was eventually rescheduled as part of a day/night doubleheader August 16—despite the fact that the teams had a common off day August 15, they apparently preferred having that off day and playing two the next day.

With the weather still lousy (45 degrees, 12 mile per hour wind blowing in), Arrieta took care of the Brewers on April 28, though any thought of back-to-back no-hitters lasted exactly five pitches before Villar led off the game with a single. The Cubs won, 7–2, to sweep the brief two-game set, and then the Braves came to town for three afternoon games.

The Cubs entered the series 16–5. The Braves arrived in Chicago 5–17, having just broken an eight-game losing streak by beating the Red Sox. How bad were the Braves? It wasn't even the end of April, and that was their second losing streak of at least eight games.

So this should be an easy sweep, right?

Well, no, because baseball.

The weather for the afternoon game Friday, April 29, wasn't really any better than it had been earlier in the week: 44 degrees at game time with another wind blowing in. And the Braves played the Cubs tough, keeping the score tied, 1–1, entering the bottom of the eighth. But that's where the Braves bullpen showed the Wrigley faithful why Atlanta had started the season so poorly.

Matt Szczur had entered the game for defensive purposes, replacing Jorge Soler in left field in the top of the inning, a wise move in a 1–1 tie. He might not even have come to bat in the bottom of the eighth except for an extended Cubs rally that started with a pinch-double by Tommy La Stella, who had taken quite well to his bench role. Dexter Fowler tried to sacrifice La Stella to third, but Braves reliever Jim Johnson threw to third to get La Stella, and you could see Fowler's frustration as he stood on first base. But Jason Heyward walked, and Ben Zobrist loaded the bases with a single. Anthony Rizzo was next to the plate, and he singled, scoring Fowler. That alone would have been enough to win the game, as it turned out. But Szczur was up next, and he smacked a ball into the bleachers for his first career grand slam. The wind had died down just enough for that ball to reach the seats. A couple of innings earlier, it might have been knocked down.

The look on Szczur's face as he rounded the bases told the story. He'd worked so hard from his days as a Villanova football player, choosing baseball over football and finally securing a place as a valuable bench player for the 2016 Cubs. I was really happy for him.

Best of all for Szczur, Cubs security folks tracked down the bleacher fan who caught the ball, and I presume it was exchanged for some Cubs swag.

More rain greeted the morning of Saturday, April 30; nevertheless, I trekked to Wrigley Field anyway, hoping the Cubs would get the proverbial "window" to play on that chilly afternoon. I hadn't been standing outside the bleacher entrance for more than 10 minutes, about an hour before the gates were scheduled to open, when a steady stream of concession gameday employees walked by, all telling us to "Go home, the game's been called!" Confirming this via Twitter, I happily spent the rest of the final day of April indoors. Since the Braves, as an outside-the-division opponent, weren't scheduled to return to Wrigley the rest of the year, the game was eventually rescheduled for a mutual off day, July 7, just before the Braves were to return to Chicago . . . to play the White Sox.

Losing that off day would loom important later in the summer. But for now, the Cubs headed into May with baseball's best record, 17–5, and a three-game lead in the NL Central.

Chapter 5

May: Continuing the Roar

The calendar turned to May, and the rain, at last, stopped. That didn't turn the weather in Chicago any warmer, though. Game-time temperature for the Cubs and Braves at Wrigley on Sunday, May 1, was 44 degrees, with the wind blowing in from center field at 14 miles per hour.

At the time the Braves came to Wrigley Field, they had a bizarre home/road split: they'd gone 1–12 at home, but 4–5 on the road, including a split at Fenway Park in Boston.

Which is why it shouldn't have been a surprise when the Cubs, riding the best record in baseball, lost their first game of May to the awful Braves. Even so, one of the best things about the 2016 Cubs was that even when they seem utterly defeated, they came back. Trailing 3–0 in the bottom of the eighth, they got a nicely-placed bunt single by Matt Szczur, who eventually scored to make it 3–1 on a double by Dexter Fowler. Kris Bryant singled in Fowler, and it was 3–2.

Fowler got tagged hard as he slid into second on that double and had to be looked over by the training staff as he got up slowly, but in the end, he seemed fine for the rest of the game.

The Cubs tied the game in the bottom of the ninth when Ben Zobrist walked and Braves closer (and former Cub) Arodys Vizcaino hurled an attempted pickoff in the general direction of the right-field bullpen. Eventually Addison Russell singled him in, and it was 3–3.

On to extras the game went, the Cubs' first foray beyond nine innings in 2016. Hector Rondon had come into this one with an 0.00 ERA in seven innings (and had struck out 12 of the 23 batters he'd faced), but even good relievers get touched up every now and again, and this wasn't Hector's day. Two singles and a sacrifice fly gave the Braves a run. Even then, the Cubs got the potential tying run on base on a two-out walk to Bryant in the bottom of the 10th, but Anthony Rizzo flied deep to left to end it.

As I said, give the Cubs credit for coming back to tie this one. Lesser teams wouldn't have even been able to do that. And even the best teams are going to lose around 60 games. So I chalked this one up to "one of those 60."

Winning teams often bring odd folks to the ballpark, and this day saw a very strange group of men inhabiting the bleachers, nine in all, a full team's worth. They were all dressed in 1908-era Cubs uniforms, which is strange enough, but what made them seem peculiar was the white makeup on their faces and black around their eyes. . . . kind of a Zombie Cubs look.

It was just . . . weird.

With a successful (albeit rain-shortened) 3–1 homestand complete, the Cubs headed to Pittsburgh for what had been anticipated as a big series for both teams, the first meeting of the year with the Pirates. It would be the first time the teams played since the 2015 wild-card game, also at PNC Park. The two rainouts at Wrigley had scratched the potential pitching rematch of the wild-card game, Jake Arrieta (who'd just been named NL Pitcher of the Month for April) vs. Gerrit Cole, though both were still slated to throw in the series.

The Pirates barely showed up. The entire series was a mismatch, swept by the Cubs, who outscored their hosts, 20–5, in the three games. In the opener, Andrew McCutchen homered off Jason Hammel in the first inning, but by the time the Pirates scored again, they were trailing, 6–1, thanks to a couple of long-sequence offensive innings. In the third, Dexter Fowler led off with a walk and was doubled in by Anthony Rizzo. Ben Zobrist's single scored Rizzo, and the Cubs led, 2–1.

Four more runs scored in the fifth, all after two were out. The second out was a sacrifice fly that scored Kris Bryant, who had walked. Then the Cubs loaded the bases on a hit-by-pitch (Addison Russell) and another walk (Matt Szczur). David Ross drove in a pair with a single, and when Ross took off for second, Szczur scored.

Somewhere in this sequence, Szczur suffered a hamstring injury that sent him to the disabled list. Hamstrings can be tricky, and this injury kept Szczur, who was off to an excellent start to his season, out for almost three weeks.

Very few saw this game, as the 18,376 announced attendance apparently included quite a number of ticket holders who were attending a Pittsburgh Penguins playoff game about a mile away at the Consol Energy Center. Perhaps a third of that count was actually inside PNC Park; many left when the Cubs took that fifth-inning lead.

The other two games of the series weren't any better for the hosts. The Cubs won the second game, 7–1, behind more stellar pitching by Jake Arrieta (seven innings of shutout ball) and completed the sweep with excellent pitching from Jon Lester (5 ⅔ innings, also no runs allowed). Dating back to 2015 and including the wild-card game victory, this made for seven consecutive wins for the Cubs at PNC Park. The somewhat-dazed hosts, who had thought they would compete with the Cubs for the NL Central title, were a distant second, six games back after just 26 games played in which the Cubs had gone 20–6.

During this win, Lester, for the second straight season, made a play in which, after fielding a comebacker, he flung his entire glove, with baseball securely inside, to Rizzo for an out. Rizzo had the presence of mind to throw his own mitt away before catching Lester's glove, and he cradled the whole thing as if he were protecting a newborn baby, making sure the baseball, which had started to come out of Lester's glove, stayed inside.

The players, as I mentioned earlier, do many monotonous fielding drills during spring training. In all the drills I watched, though,
they never practiced that glove toss, but it somehow seemed pretty
natural for Rizzo. On what the Cubs termed the "minimalist zany
suit trip," this was sort of a "minimalist zany play," and hey, whatever it takes for Lester to get outs on baseballs that are hit his way.

Joe Maddon invented the "minimalist zany suit trip" as yet
another one of his fun events to take his players' minds off the long
grind of the season. And the Cubs did significant Internet research
to find the wackiest-looking suits they would wear not only on the
flights, but as often as they could while out and about in Pittsburgh.
These included John Lackey and Travis Wood in camo suits, Kyle
Hendricks in red plaid, Kris Bryant in a red-white-and-blue number resembling the American flag (Anthony Rizzo had a similar
idea, only with shorts), Joe Maddon in a baby-blue suit with red
roses, and Clayton Richard as the Riddler from Batman.

It certainly must have been a lot more fun to do this given the
sweep.

And then the Washington Nationals came to Wrigley Field for
a four-game weekend series, and the Cubs broke Bryce Harper.

The Nats' 19–8 record entering the series was second in the
major leagues only to the Cubs' and the reigning National League
MVP was off to a fine start, hitting .266/.372/.649 with 10 home
runs in those 27 games.

And Maddon and the Cubs had clearly decided that they simply weren't going to let Harper defeat them.

In the opener, Kyle Hendricks threw six shutout innings and
Ben Zobrist homered in a 5–2 win. One of Hendricks's best quali-
ties is his command. He issued two walks, both to Harper, who
eventually singled off Hendricks with two out in the sixth. With the
Cubs ahead, 5–0, Travis Wood threw the ninth and walked Harper
leading off. Eventually, Jayson Werth homered to make it 5–2, the
final score.

Friday, May 6, it turned suddenly summer at Wrigley Field,
with the temperature hitting 80 just a week after everyone had

shivered through a 40-degree weekend. And Ben Zobrist's bat was getting as hot as the weather. Zobrist homered twice, and the Cubs ran out to an 8–2 win after seven innings. A bit of shaky relief pitching by Clayton Richard and Justin Grimm gave the Nats a four-run eighth to make it close, but Hector Rondon finished it out with a 1-2-3 ninth. For Zobrist, it was his third straight game with three or more RBI, the first Cub to do that since Sammy Sosa in 2003.

Harper went 0-for-3 in this game with a pair of walks and a run scored. It was the only time in the series where he had more than one official at-bat.

The Cubs had now won five straight and were 22–6. In addition to that being the best start for any Cubs team since 1907, it was the best start by any National League team since the 1977 Dodgers also began 22–6. Two more recent teams that roared through their leagues (the 114-win 1998 Yankees and the 116-win 2001 Mariners) also began their years 22–6.

It wouldn't stop there, but Harper finally was halted. The Cubs had to come from behind to take the third game in the series. Trailing 4–2 going into the bottom of the sixth, the Cubs got an RBI single from Addison Russell to make it 4–3, and after they loaded the bases, Ryan Kalish singled in two more.

Who?

Ryan Kalish was an old favorite of Theo & Co. Drafted in the ninth round in 2006 by Theo's Red Sox, Kalish never made it as a regular due to injuries. He had been completely out of baseball in 2013 when Theo signed him to a minor-league deal before the 2014 season, and he played in 57 games for the big-league Cubs that year. Again released and out of baseball in 2015, he was signed for 2016 after spring camp had already begun, played a handful of games at Triple-A Iowa, and was called up to the Cubs due to Szczur's injury.

And on this May afternoon he came up with a key pinch hit, driving in two runs that would put the Cubs ahead. Kalish played in only seven games for the 2016 Cubs, going 2-for-7 at the plate. He didn't even get a September recall, but he'll get a championship ring along with all the other contributors to this title season. For that, he should be remembered.

Harper did drive in one run in this game, eventually won by the Cubs, 8–5, and he walked his other three times at the plate, once intentionally. But that was nothing compared to the Sunday series finale.

The Nats went out to an early lead with single runs in the third, fourth, and fifth off Jake Arrieta, while the Cubs scored just once in that time frame. One of those Nats runs was scored by Harper, after a third-inning walk. He scored on a double. By then he had already walked twice. He was intentionally walked in the fourth—three walks in four innings! In the sixth, with Trevor Cahill pitching, Harper wasn't walked; instead, Cahill hit him with his first offering, which seemed to irritate Harper no end.

When Cahill's spot in the order came up in the seventh, he was left in to bat for himself, a .102 career hitter entering the game. Naturally, he singled up the middle, and after a Dexter Fowler single and sacrifice by Jason Heyward (backward, right? The pitcher's supposed to bunt and the outfielder is supposed to hit!), the Cubs tied the game on a two-run single by Kris Bryant. Then the bullpen got to work on keeping it that way. Harper drew walk number four in the eighth, where he was stranded. Neither team scored in the ninth, and on the game went to extras.

How serious were the Cubs about not letting Harper beat them? In the 10th, the Nats had runners on first and second with two out, and Maddon ordered another intentional walk to Harper—even with first base occupied. Ryan Zimmerman cooperated by hitting a line drive right to Dexter Fowler to end the inning.

Really, it was Zimmerman's failures that set up all the walks to Harper. Zimmerman, who had gone 7-for-14 with four doubles in the Nats' series against the Royals that preceded their visit to Wrigley, had been shut down in the first three games by Cubs pitchers: 1-for-12. So they likely figured they could just keep doing this, and it worked.

In the 11th, Heyward singled and Bryant doubled into the gap, but a great relay from Nats center fielder Michael Taylor to shortstop Danny Espinosa to catcher Wilson Ramos nailed Heyward. Joe Maddon challenged the play (based on the collision rule), but the review crew upheld the out and the game continued.

Again, Harper came to bat with runners on first and second and two out in the 12th, and just as the time before, he was intentionally passed. Zimmerman grounded to third to end the inning.

Mind you, the Cubs weren't really doing anything to help people get to Mother's Day dinners on time (including Miriam and me, though we did make it close to our reserved time for dinner with her mom). That is, until Javier Baez hit a 2–2 pitch into the left-field bleachers for a walkoff home run. It was the Cubs' first walkoff victory of 2016, something that might surprise you until you realize that of the 22 wins that preceded this one, 13 of them were by five or more runs, "blowouts" per baseball-reference. com's definition. Overall in the 2016 regular season, the Cubs were 42–13 in blowouts, a testament to both the offensive juggernaut they became and the pitching staff's excellent work.

As for Harper? In the four-game series, he went 1-for-4 with 13 walks. This performance led to all sorts of records and statistical oddities:

- Here's the sequence of Harper's 19 plate appearances in the series: BB, BB, single, BB, groundout, K, K, BB, BB, sacrifice fly, BB, IBB, BB, BB, IBB, HBP, BB, IBB, IBB.
- Per STATS LLC, Harper was the only player in at least 40 years to draw two intentional walks in extra innings with first AND second base occupied both times.
- It was just the fourth time since 1913 (as far as bb-ref's database goes) that a player had walked six times in a game, and the first since 1999 (Jeff Bagwell).
- With the six walks and HBP in the series finale, Harper became the first player in the past 100 years to reach base seven times in a game without an official at-bat.

- The 13 walks were the most ever for any player in a four-game series.

The whole thing must have driven Nats manager Dusty "Walks Clog The Bases" Baker crazy. But the Cubs had a four-game sweep and a seven-game winning streak. And Harper's performance going forward from this game suffered. Though he hit 24 home runs and drew 108 walks (12 percent of them in these four games alone), his overall numbers dropped considerably from his 2015 MVP performance. I like to think all the walks messed with his mind enough that he couldn't get back on track for the rest of the season. He didn't hit much in the Cubs' series against the Nats in mid-June in Washington, either: 2-for-11, though with only three walks.

Harper did endear himself to at least one Chicagoan as the Nats departed on their team bus. He reportedly got off the bus with quite a bit of money contributed by him and his teammates and gave it to a homeless woman who was sitting under a tree on Sheffield Avenue.

Good for you, Bryce Harper. Many don't like him. I do. Not only is he a great baseball player, but he's a breath of fresh air for the game. If MLB wants to get younger people interested in baseball, they should promote him. Big-time.

Meanwhile, the Cubs had to wait an extra day to try to extend their seven-game winning streak, as a scheduled Monday, May 9, date with the San Diego Padres was rained out, called at 7:10 p.m., shortly after the first pitch was scheduled to be thrown. It was rescheduled for a 12:05 p.m. start Wednesday, May 11, before the night game already on the docket, making for the entire series to be played in a span of about 27 hours.

That proved to be a bit too much even for the high-flying Cubs. They did extend their great start to 25–6 with an 8–7 win May 10, led by a 4-for-4 night from Ben Zobrist, who had a fantastic month of May. A bit of sketchy relief pitching in the late innings by Justin Grimm and Adam Warren made this game closer than it had to be, and this one also nearly got rained out. Smartphone radars showed angry red and yellow blobs just south of Chicago's Loop, but nothing ever got to the North Side even as the south and west suburbs got clobbered with heavy rain.

And then the makeup game happened, and the Cubs did something they hadn't done at all in the season's first 31 games: lose two in a row. Yes, swept in a doubleheader by the lowly Padres, who would wind up a 94-loss team, in last place in their division.

Because baseball. The Cubs had won eight in a row entering the doubleheader, and appeared headed to consecutive win number nine, until the Padres pushed across four runs in the seventh. That was mostly thanks to a bad outing by Pedro Strop, who had been scored on in just two of his previous 16 appearances. The 7–4 loss was witnessed by an announced "crowd" of 34,508, and I put "crowd" in quotes because on a coolish, foggy afternoon, there were probably fewer than half that many in the house due to the last-minute rescheduling of this makeup game. Word on the street was that bleacher tickets were going for about half the season-ticket price of $27.

I spent the in-between-games time at my friend Ken's place across the street from Wrigley Field writing up a recap for Bleed Cubbie Blue and then headed in for Game 2, which saw the Cubs offense completely sputter and die. Drew Pomeranz, who'd wind up finishing the year in Boston, shut down the Cubs for six innings, and the Padres bullpen didn't give up anything either. Finishing off was Fernando Rodney, whom the Cubs rescued from the scrap heap at the end of 2015, and whom the Padres installed as closer after spring training 2016. He, too, ended the 2016 season elsewhere (Miami). The only run scored on a home run by Christian Bethancourt that flew over the brand-new NUVEEN advertising sign in left field.

The defeat marked the Cubs' first 1–0 loss since July 10, 2015, when the White Sox hung one on them at Wrigley. They hadn't been swept in a doubleheader since July 8, 2014, at Cincinnati, nor in a doubleheader at home since a couple of weeks before that by the Nationals on June 28, 2014.

The 2016 Pirates were the cure to many Cubs ills during the season, and the weekend set with them at Wrigley was no exception. The Cubs brought out the big bats in the first two games, outscoring the visitors from Pittsburgh, 17–6 (9–4 on Friday and 8–2 on Saturday), with homers hit by David Ross (the 99th of his career), Kris Bryant, and Addison Russell (one each day).

The Cubs finally lost one to the Pirates after winning the first five of the season in the Sunday affair, as Gerrit Cole outdueled Jon Lester. The 2–1 win had Cole confident, or perhaps I should say overconfident; he told reporters after the game: "I don't really think they're the best team in baseball, so it's just one game at a time."

If the Cubs had wound up playing the Pirates in a postseason series, that probably would have become a major meme, bulletin-board fodder, and dissected by the talking heads on ESPN and MLB Network.

Instead, I get to quote Cole and say he was wrong—way wrong. The Cubs were indeed the best team in baseball in 2016 and Cole took in the playoffs from his sofa, if he watched them at all.

The loss didn't seem to mean that much, but the Cubs bused up to Milwaukee after an off day and had a clunker of a series at Miller Park.

Maybe it was my fault. I wound up seeing five Cubs regular-season road games in 2016, and they lost all of them (two in Milwaukee, two at the Cell, and one in San Francisco).

The only win in the Miller Park series was a 13-inning, 2–1 affair in which the Cubs tied the game with two out in the ninth and Travis Wood, who generally handles the bat well, drove in the winning run with a bases-loaded walk.

But that wasn't the game I saw. Instead, I sat through a snore-fest the next afternoon in which Dexter Fowler led off the game with a home run but the Cubs had only five other hits and blew a 2–0 lead. Fowler nearly gave the Cubs the lead in the ninth when he lofted a long fly ball to right with two men on base and one out, but Ramon Flores caught it at the wall, disappointing the crowd, which was nearly half Cubs fans.

It was the Cubs' first road series loss of 2016, and unfortunately they wouldn't have to wait too long for the next one.

I've never understood major-league scheduling, and I sure didn't get this one. The Cubs and Giants both had off days Monday, May 16. While the Cubs had a bus ride from Chicago to Milwaukee, the Giants had a short-hop flight from Phoenix to San Diego, where they played the Padres on the same three days the Cubs were at Miller Park. The Giants had to have May 16 off because otherwise their schedule would have violated the rule that states no team can play on more than 20 consecutive days. But the Cubs didn't have that issue and had to fly from Milwaukee to San Francisco and play the next day, two time zones away.

Thanks, schedule makers, for nothing.

It didn't affect the Cubs on the first day on the West Coast, as they beat the Giants, 8–1, and in the game Jason Heyward slammed into the center-field wall at AT&T Park after making a diving, sliding catch on the warning track. Giants broadcaster Mike Krukow, who's seen more games at that park than just about anyone, called it one of the greatest he'd ever seen in the park.

It appeared Heyward might have separated or dislocated a shoulder, but it turned out he simply had a "contusion." He missed three games.

The Cubs tossed away the game Saturday, May 21, in San Francisco by letting Jon Lester, who had nothing, stay in too long. He threw 75 pitches and recorded only eight outs, and the 2 2/3-inning outing was his shortest as a Cub. The score was "just" 5–3, but the game never seemed that close; and worse, I thought the Fox broadcast team was awful. Matt Vasgersian completely missed one play, when Anthony Rizzo fielded a ground ball with a runner on first. Rizzo briefly thought about throwing to second but didn't, taking the out at first. Vasgersian started talking about "getting the lead runner" before realizing his mistake and making fun of himself, which I guess is all right, except he'd have been better off just watching the play in the first place.

Later in the broadcast, Eric Karros, who was a popular Cub in his one season on the North Side, began talking about the "varied starting times" at Wrigley Field, which was the case when he played there in 2003, but most definitely is not the case anymore, as Joe Maddon influenced the business side of Cubs management to have more consistent starting times for 2016 (primarily 7:05 at night, 1:20 for day games, with only a couple of exceptions). If a broadcaster is going to talk about things like this on national TV, he should at least get his facts straight.

Beyond that, the video shaders (the guys who adjust the light levels when the TV cameras move from bright light into shade at live events like this) seemed to be having trouble adjusting the camera levels on some of the shots early in the game. The fact that the Giants were wearing black jerseys with black numbers that had thin orange outlines didn't help. Those are almost unreadable unless you're standing up close to the players, and fans at the park aren't. Marketing departments make these things up to try and juice "alternate jersey" sales, with no thought of how they actually look to people watching the games. When the Giants had similar jerseys for several years in spring training, even the team broadcasters complained, saying they couldn't read them and couldn't figure out who some of the players were. No matter, Giants marketing said, they were going to keep them anyway.

I'm glad the Cubs don't do things like that.

The Cubs lost a tough one in a Sunday night ESPN broadcast with Kyle Hendricks facing Madison Bumgarner. Hendricks hung in with MadBum for five innings, until the Giants lefthander drove in the only run of the game with a double over Jorge Soler's head in left field. The Cubs might have been jobbed out of a hit in the eighth inning. Javier Baez tried to reach by bunt and slid out of the way of Brandon Belt's tag, reaching first base before he was tagged. He was ruled to have run out of the baseline—but runners are allowed to do this in trying to avoid a tag of that type. It did appear that Baez left the baseline, but not by much, and in such a circumstance a player is allowed to do so. Unfortunately, this kind of play is not reviewable, which is why Joe Maddon raced out of the dugout, almost wagging a pen in umpire Dana DeMuth's face. You could tell Joe was livid. I suspect DeMuth knew he made the wrong call, which is why Maddon wasn't tossed.

Hopefully, the committee in charge of deciding which plays are reviewable will add plays like this to the list in future years. There's no reason it couldn't be, even though this is a judgment call.

So the Cubs had lost back-to-back series for the first time in 2016, and then it was time for another trip to St. Louis.

And the first game resulted in the first three-game losing streak for the 2016 Cubs, and in about the worst way you could imagine: a walkoff homer by Randal Grichuk off Adam Warren when the Cubs were one strike away from sending the game into extras.

Before that, John Lackey had blown a 3–1 lead when he gave up a two-run homer to Matt Adams in the seventh. That was a pinch-homer, the Cardinals' ninth of the year—in only 45 games! (They eventually set a major-league record with 17 pinch homers. The Cubs had two.)

That loss, however, would be the Cubs' last for more than a week. The Cubs pounded out 15 hits in a 12–3 blowout in the second game of the series, a contest that featured Justin Grimm ending the eighth inning with a no-look, between-the-legs grab of a comebacker. Said Grimm after the game: "I've always wanted to do that, whether it's behind the back, between the legs. I actually told the umpire that."

The third game, a 9–8 win, began to show some cracks in the previously impermeable Jake Arrieta facade. Jake allowed seven hits and threw 93 pitches and didn't get out of the fifth inning. The four runs off him were the most he'd allowed in nearly a year. He wasn't helped by plate umpire C. B. Bucknor's characteristically weird strike zone, but after the Cubs built leads of 6–2 and 9–4, they had to hang on with the tying and winning runs on base as

Hector Rondon knocked down a ground ball appeared headed up the middle for the win.

Despite Jake's shakiness, the Cubs tied a major-league record by winning the 23rd consecutive game started by him.

And then the Cubs came home and started roaring through East and West division opponents.

The Phillies were up first. As part of my Bleed Cubbie Blue series previews, I often ask the manager of the opposition's site to write a bit about their team, so my readers can get information from someone who knows the team well.

Liz Roscher runs the Phillies site The Good Phight. And she is hilarious. Here's just a bit of what she wrote about her team:

> I'm back to talk about the Phillies again, only this time, things are different. These aren't the same Phillies you split a four-game series with last September. And they're even more different than the Phillies who swept and no-hit you last July.

> You understand why I had to mention that, right? I just had to. I can't not.

> They are better, at least a little bit, than they were in 2015. But the leap that the Cubs took between last season and this season is a regular human step to the Phillies' dainty doll step. Imagine you take a regular step forward. And now imagine a G.I. Joe toy taking a step forward next to you. That's the difference. The Phillies will get there, but they certainly won't get there by this weekend.

> And now for the guys who if I could, I would replace with the inflatable noodle men you see outside of car dealerships. Ryan Howard has to top this list. It hurts, but he's earned it. His average has been under .200

more days than it's been above. He has a .105 average in May, which is just six hits. Six! Watching him bat is not even torturous, it's just aggressively sad. And then there's Peter Bourjos, who has started the vast, vast majority of games this year despite sucking like a vacuum with a .203 average. Manager Pete Mackanin has said that Bourjos starts because of his defense, but he's actually not very good at that either, and honestly wouldn't two inflatable noodle men be more entertaining?

Please be gentle with the Phillies. Please. Please, please, please.

The Cubs were not gentle with the Phillies. No, not at all, even though she asked nicely. Sorry, Liz. They swept them and outscored them, 17–5, and the games weren't as close as that total score might indicate.

The contest of Friday, May 27, was played through three heavy rainfalls, the last of which caused an hour's worth of delay in the seventh inning. Perhaps 3,000 of the announced house of 38,941 stuck around to the end. (Of course I did. You have to ask?)

The first rain began not long after the bottom of the first inning started, and they played through it, obviously informed that it would pass through quickly, and it did (it rained hard for maybe 10 minutes). Ben Zobrist, who was nearing the end of an amazing May in which he'd wind up hitting .406/.483/.653 (41-for-101) with seven doubles and six home runs, doubled in a run, and Jorge Soler made it 2–0.

The Phillies tied the game in the third, thanks partly to a rare drop of a routine fly ball by Dexter Fowler, but then the Cubs started hitting home runs.

Soler parked one that hit about a third of the way up the left-field video board; and following a flyout, a walk, and a single, David Ross reached a milestone with his 100th career homer.

Ross became the first Cubs player to hit the new NUVEEN sign in left field—and the company had announced it'd make a $10,000 donation to Cubs Charities for every homer that hit the sign, so it was more valuable than just the three runs.

Ross became the oldest Cub to homer since Gary Gaetti in 1999, and Kris Bryant completed the homer barrage with his 11th of the season.

Saturday's game gave us a hint of how good Kyle Hendricks was to become in 2016. He threw a complete-game five-hitter, with the only Phillies run scoring on a wild pitch on strike three in the top of the ninth. The only reason there was a baserunner at all in that inning was that Jason Heyward and Ben Zobrist let a catchable ball drop between them for a double by Freddy Galvis leading off the ninth. Without having heard anything from either of those players, I suspect it was simply a case of each of them thinking the other had the play; after the game they confirmed it was hard to hear each other with the large crowd energized for a win. Galvis advanced to third on a groundout. Hendricks then struck out Ryan Howard, but Miguel Montero dropped the third strike.

Hendricks looked Galvis back to third and then fired to Anthony Rizzo at first base to retire Howard. But as that was happening, Galvis took off for the plate and Rizzo's throw came in just a bit late, ruining Hendricks's shutout. He recovered and got Cameron Rupp to ground to third base to end the game, an excellent performance by Hendricks. If not for the missed pop fly, Hendricks might have thrown "a Maddux" (defined as a complete-game shutout with fewer than 100 pitches). As it was, it still was a rarity: the first Cubs complete game thrown at Wrigley Field by anyone not named "Arrieta" since Jeff Samardzija had one against the Nationals in August 2013.

At two hours, 18 minutes, the game was kind of a throwback to an earlier, Fergie Jenkins-style era, where starting pitchers went the distance and fans got to head home before 4:00. I rather like those.

Sunday, the Cubs completed the sweep and ran their winning streak to five behind more home run power. Miguel Montero became the first Cubs player to hit the right-field video board in the second inning, smacking one off the bottom of the board that didn't appear to need any help from the west wind blowing out to right.

Ben Zobrist, still on his May tear, extended a hitting streak to 15 games with a three-run shot in the fifth that did need some wind assistance, just barely making the basket.

The 7–2 win (it was 7–0 before the Phillies hit a couple of consolation late-inning solo homers) produced the first Cubs sweep of the Phillies at Wrigley Field since July 28–30, 1995. The losing pitcher in the last of those games was Cubs TV analyst Jim Deshaies, who was pounded for six runs in fewer than two innings. It turned out to be the last game of Deshaies's career, as he was released the next day.

And 21 years later, he got to broadcast the game that provided a match to that long-ago Cubs sweep.

The Dodgers came to town for a four-game set that began on Monday, Memorial Day, so the pregame was filled with festivities, including a giant American flag that covered the entire outfield at Wrigley. And the Cubs invited Ben Zobrist's wife, Julianna, to sing the National Anthem. This wasn't just a favor done for a player, either; Julianna Zobrist is a well-known singer of Christian pop music, and her song "Alive" is heard every time Ben comes to the plate at Wrigley Field. She was asked about that in an interview with the Chicago Tribune around this time and said: "I think it's hilarious.... I have told him every single season: 'Babe, you really don't have to choose my song. It would probably be way cooler for you to choose Jack White or other artists.' But he's like, 'No, I like your music the best.' So I always put it in his hands. It's not a marketing ploy on my end. He's got his deal and I've got mine."

Truth be told, I normally don't care for many of the anthem singers I hear at ballparks. Some of them embellish the melody to a point where it's unrecognizable, or hold the word "Free" for 20 seconds (granted, an impressive feat of breath control, but a little much), instead of just doing the song straight, as an anthem. As some friends of mine and I once agreed, "If it takes you longer than 90 seconds to sing the National Anthem, you're doing it wrong."

Julianna Zobrist's rendition was respectful and stirring, and her voice carried it well. I found myself wishing they'd invite her back to do it more often.

Two innings into the game, Jason Hammel collapsed while warming up and had to leave with what was later diagnosed as hamstring cramping. This is a problem that Hammel had suffered on other occasions in his Cubs tenure, and later in the year the team would come up with a creative solution.

But on this day, they needed the bullpen to step up, and up Travis Wood stepped, throwing four perfect innings of relief, striking out four. In fact, the collective Cubs relief corps that day of Wood, Justin Grimm, Pedro Strop, and Hector Rondon threw seven perfect innings, striking out eight of the total 21 hitters they faced. Hammel had allowed a two-out single to Justin Turner and a walk to Adrian Gonzalez in the first inning, allowing him to joke, "I ruined the no-hitter," after the Cubs had won, 2–0, on RBI hits by Jason Heyward and Anthony Rizzo in the fifth. The Cubs' sixth straight win on a gloriously sunny day was nearly perfect in every way. It also produced something unusual: the first 4:05 p.m. game time in Wrigley Field history. This had been requested by the Dodgers after they were scheduled to play a Sunday night game the previous evening in New York.

Normally, the Cubs would probably have agreed to switch the Monday game to 7:05 and swap out one of the later night games in the series, but Cubs management has always liked to have holiday games in the daytime (save the 2015 Fourth of July game in which they actually set off postgame fireworks outside Wrigley). So 4:05 it was, making the series have starts at 4:05, 7:05, 7:05, and 1:20, not exactly what Joe Maddon had in mind for "consistency," though it should be said this was the only time this happened in 2016.

The winning streak ended at six on the month's last day. The game was delayed by 27 minutes at the start by moderate-to-heavy rain that started about 4:00 and lasted till about 6:30, after which it took the grounds crew a while to prepare the field for play. At one point around 5:15, Cubs security folks cleared the bleachers and other exposed areas due to lightning expected in the area, though none even materialized. Once the game started no more rain fell, though it got quite cool and a lake breeze developed. Cubs hitters lofted several fly balls that looked like they might head toward the outfield walls or the seats, but the ball was simply not carrying in the heavy air.

Jake Arrieta threw seven shutout innings, but LA's Scott Kazmir matched him, and Joe pulled Jake after 107 pitches and four walks, and Maddon later said he'd have left Jake in if not for the walks. Clayton Richard, a mostly forgotten man in the season's early going—he hadn't pitched in a week when called on for the eighth—got hit, and hit hard, by the only three batters he faced, and by the time Adam Warren finished up that inning the Cubs trailed, 3–0, and Warren and Trevor Cahill made it 5–0 after Corey Seager absolutely destroyed a baseball that wound up in the right-field party patio.

There was one oddity in this loss that's worth noting: after a double switch when Cahill entered the game, Tommy La Stella wound up at third base and 6-foot-5 Kris Bryant moved to short-stop for an inning, in the process, according to stats guru Chris Kamka, becoming the tallest shortstop in Cubs history. (Previous record holders, at 6-3: Jason Smith, Alex Arias, Andre Rodgers, and Roy Smalley Sr.)

Despite the defeat, the Cubs wrapped a successful May at 18–10; coming off their 17–5 April, the 35–15 record put them 6 1/2 games in first place.

Chapter 6

June: Swoon

June.

Once upon a time, back in the early 1970s, Cubs fans became accustomed to what was termed the "June Swoon" from teams that roared out to early leads, only to flop once the weather turned warm.

It happened in 1970 (10–18, first at the beginning of the month, second when it ended), 1972 (14–17), and a bit delayed in 1973 (17–13 in June, but 8–19 in July).

This year, though? What could happen to a team that entered June 35–15?

Plenty, as it turned out. At the end of June and beginning of July, the Cubs team that had gotten off to the best start (47–20) since 1918 suddenly looked like the worst team in baseball.

This is not hyperbole. The 2012 Cubs, 101-game losers in the first year of Theo Epstein's rebuild, at one point lost 16 of 20 games. The 2016 Cubs, champions of all they surveyed, lost 15 of 20. It was inexplicable.

I'll get to that, but first, the roll the Cubs were on ending May continued into early June. Jon Lester's second pitch of the first game of June was launched into the bleachers by Kiké Hernandez, but after that Lester slammed the door on the Dodgers. He allowed only three other hits, didn't walk anyone, struck out 10, and retired the final 15 Dodgers he faced in throwing a complete-game win. Kris Bryant provided all the offense the Cubs needed with a two-run homer into the shrubbery in center field.

In throwing his CG, Lester put some more "not since" numbers on the board:

He became the first Cubs pitcher to allow a leadoff home run and no other runs in a complete game since Larry French did it July 26, 1940, against the Giants . . . nearly 76 years earlier. And he became the first Cubs left-hander with a complete game and no walks since Steve Wilson did it July 15, 1990, against the Dodgers (Wilson also struck out 10).

It's those kinds of numbers that had many of us dropping our jaws all summer. These were literally things, many of them, that had not been seen in our lifetime, for some in their parents' lifetime.

On the second day of the month, the Cubs completed a series win over the Dodgers by a 7–2 score. Summer, at last, seemed to have arrived in Chicago with brilliant sunshine and 78-degree temperatures, and Kyle Hendricks began to show the form that would make him a Cy Young Award candidate. Hendricks threw eight innings, allowed just three hits and two runs, while striking out six with his "fastball" that barely touched 90 on Wrigley's pitch speed meter. Meanwhile, the Cubs hit four home runs off 19-year-old Dodgers rookie Julio Urias, who was making his second big-league start. One of those homers, by Kris Bryant, hit about a third of the way up the left-field video board. Bryant's made a habit out of hitting that board, and one day I think he'll become the first Cub to hit a baseball over the board. In the meantime, I hope Tom Ricketts doesn't dock Bryant's pay for replacing any of the LED panels that get damaged by his power show!

The Diamondbacks were next in town, the first team against whom the Cubs would complete their season series and not see again until 2017.

John Lackey, perhaps intent on matching Hendricks's performance of the previous afternoon, shut out the D-backs for 6⅔ innings, striking out nine, and the blanking was completed by

Adam Warren, Travis Wood, and Justin Grimm. Jason Heyward, Javier Baez, and Ben Zobrist contributed key defensive plays to help keep Arizona off the board, and the Cubs got a pair of two-run extra-base hits in a five-run eighth, one from Baez, the other from Addison Russell, to blow the game open for a 6–0 win.

At the time it was the Cubs' 20th "blowout" win, as defined by baseball-reference.com, a win by five or more runs. On that date, three teams: Reds (19), Twins (16), and Braves (16) had fewer than 20 total wins.

That afternoon, our bleacher crew in the left-field corner was joined by CSN Chicago's Kelly Crull and a gigantic crane holding a small, handheld-type TV camera. Crull did some updates before and during the game and was friendly to us, at one point wondering whether I'd swiped her clipboard (oddly, the clipboard I use for holding my scorecard looked nearly identical to the one she had her notes on). She, and the ginormous crane that had at least 350 pounds of counterweights, were to return several more times during the summer.

The next day, early spring poked its head out and reminded us that Chicago summers generally don't start until July. Temperatures in the 50s, wind, and threatening clouds came before the game was able to begin. The Cubs put the tarp on the field about 12:05, but no rain fell. They took it off 50 minutes later, and the game started on time—in a steady light rain that got a little bit moderate at times, but with no lightning in the area, they decided to play through it. It stopped in the middle innings, then the skies opened up again briefly in the seventh before finally ending. With this being the final series between the two teams this year, I suppose they figured they'd play unless there was a drenching downpour or severe weather.

The game didn't start out well. Jason Hammel issued a two-out walk in the first inning, and then Jake Lamb smacked a two-run homer to give Arizona a 2–0 lead.

That turned out to be the only hit Hammel would allow in seven strong innings. Hammel also got a hit himself, a two-run single that gave the Cubs the lead in the fourth. The D-backs got back to within one at 4–3 off Pedro Strop in the eighth, but Anthony Rizzo's 13th home run of the season provided insurance for the Cubs' fourth straight win and 10th in their last 11 outings.

The Cubs were at the one-third mark of the 2016 season following this win at 39–15. Absurdly, that was a pace for 117 wins, which would have broken the all-time major-league win record, which is also the franchise record: 116, held by the 1906 Cubs. They didn't make it but they did wind up with more wins than any Cubs team had since 1910.

Watching the Diamondbacks, who unveiled no fewer than eight different uniform combinations for 2016, was kind of an odd experience on this day. Friday, it was hard to read the uniform numbers on the dark-gray road jerseys they wore. With black shirts Saturday, at least the numbers were easier to read. But with a black jersey over dark gray pants, they looked like a team full of umpires. It's just a very strange look, in my opinion.

The winning streak ended at four the next afternoon, as Patrick Corbin outdueled Jake Arrieta. The Cubs got to within 3–2 after a Javier Baez homer in the sixth, and got the tying run on base in the eighth and ninth, but could not score. Sometimes that just happens!

The loss ended Jake Arrieta's personal winning streak at 20— the last time before June 5 that he had lost a game, the Cubs had to get no-hit (by Cole Hamels in July 2015) to do it. Three of the Cubs' five pitchers on the day—Arrieta, Travis Wood, and Adam Warren—combined for 18 strikeouts, tying for the second-highest single-game total in team history. It had last been done in a nine-inning game August 26, 1998 (Kerry Wood, 16, and Rod Beck, two).

The Cubs completed a 10-game homestand with an 8–2 record and stood 22–8 at home and 17–8 on the road, and the latter was important because the team was entering a stretch of 23 out of 33 away from Wrigley Field heading into the All-Star break.

The road trip began in Philadelphia, and once again, Liz Roscher of SB Nation's The Good Phight helped me out:

> Greetings again, BCB readers. After sweeping the Phillies last week at Wrigley (**sob**) the Cubs are facing the Phillies again, but this time at Citizens Bank Park. You know the basics now after seeing them for three games, so let's get to what's happened since.
>
> First off, THANKS A WHOLE LOT. That sweep was the start of a bad run for the Phillies. After the Cubs swept them, the Nationals did the same thing, and then they split four games with the Brewers. But I'm sure this three-game series with the Cubs again is totally what they need to get back on track! Also, it's opposite day.
>
> PLEASE DON'T SWEEP THE PHILLIES, PLEASE PLEASE PLEASE, PLEASE DON'T DO IT AGAIN, I CAN'T TAKE IT PLEASE DON'T SWEEP THEM PLEEEEEEEEEEEASE.

This time, the Cubs listened to Liz's plea, but not before winning the first game of the set, 6–4. They got eight outstanding shutout innings from Jon Lester, who became the first Cubs left-hander to strike out 9 without a walk in consecutive starts during the modern era (since 1900). This game would have been a much easier win if Joe Maddon had let Lester, who'd thrown only 95 pitches, try to complete his shutout.

Instead, Justin Grimm, who didn't really need the work (he'd appeared in two of the previous three games), entered with a 6–0 lead in the ninth. He threw eight pitches, and three of them went for Phillies hits, the last a three-run homer by Freddy Galvis. This sent Hector Rondon to warm up hurriedly. Perhaps Hector wasn't properly warmed up, because his fourth pitch was launched into the seats by Tommy Joseph. Rondon did retire the next two batters and allowed a single, bringing Ryan Howard to the plate representing the tying run in a game that shouldn't have gotten anywhere near that point.

You know, the old, bad Cubs would have served up a game-tying homer to Howard. But this wasn't those old Cubs, and Ryan Howard was going through what was to be a bad and final season in Philadelphia. He hit the first pitch on the ground to Anthony Rizzo to end the game.

More important in this one was yet another hamstring injury to Jorge Soler. In the third inning, Soler singled with one out and appeared to tweak his hammy rounding first base. This is something that plagued him throughout his minor-league career, and he missed some time in 2015 with a similar injury. At first, the injury was ruled "day-to-day," but Soler would not return for two months. He had just started to get hot right before this, too, after a horrific start to his 2016 season. Hitting just .184 on May 18, Soler hit .302/.423/.581 in 16 games before this injury with three home runs.

The Cubs had to play the entire season without Kyle Schwarber and were able to use their depth to fill the hole in the lineup. Could they do the same without Soler?

The injury sent the team scrambling. They probably hadn't intended to call up Albert Almora Jr. this early, but since they needed a right-handed outfield bat, Almora joined the ball club. And two days later, Chris Coghlan, who'd been shipped to Oakland when Dexter Fowler re-signed, was reacquired from the A's for Arismendy Alcantara. Coghlan was the worst everyday player in the American League at the time of his return to the Cubs—he was hitting .146/.215/.272 in 172 plate appearances, but with five home runs. To make room for Coghlan on the 25-man roster, Tommy La Stella hit the DL with a hamstring strain. (Those aren't contagious; it just seemed so.)

A couple of months after his return, when the Cubs were playing in Oakland, Coghlan told the Tribune: "I'm so grateful I'm here. And it makes it more special with the guys I'm doing it with, the relationships I've formed here and the history we're chasing. We're chasing history, not just a World Series. And it makes the challenge that much sweeter. That's more difficult to deal with, but it makes it so precious. I wouldn't want to be on any other team."

With the Cubs' win in Philadelphia yet another impressive milestone was reached: the Cubs' lead in the division became 10 games (a 10-game lead is pretty rare in the history of the Cubs franchise). Of course, a 10-game lead in a division isn't the same as a 10-game lead was in a single league, as baseball was divided before 1969. The Cubs' 40–16 record at the time was 6 1/2 games better than the next-best team in the NL (Nationals, 34–23, and Giants, 35–24). Even that's a pretty impressive lead for early June. And the Cubs had posted a 10-game lead in any league or division just six other times in franchise history: 1906, 1907, 1910, 1918, 1929, and 2008. Every one of those years ended with postseason play.

So things were looking good, and then the Cubs made a couple of key mistakes in a 3–2 loss to the Phillies the next night. (See, Liz? The Cubs heard your pleas!)

The first was Kris Bryant's misjudgment of Freddy Galvis's long fly ball in the first inning. It might not have been an easy play, but Bryant has caught balls like this before. Galvis wound up on second base with a double and scored on a single by Maikel Franco.

The other one was more egregious, in my view. With the score 2–1 Phillies in the seventh, Carlos Ruiz singled with one out. Then he stole second base.

My jaw dropped. I mean, this is a 37-year-old catcher who had only one steal attempt this year (unsuccessful) before this game. Miguel Montero had been really bad at throwing out runners trying to steal this year: just two in 23 attempts at that point (and it got worse). The Phillies obviously scouted him well.

If Ruiz doesn't steal that base, the pitch that got away when Jimmy Paredes struck out wouldn't have mattered. Paredes wouldn't have taken first base, as it would have been occupied. Maybe Ruiz advances, maybe he doesn't, but he isn't likely to score on the single by Odubel Herrera that easily scored him from third, where he did advance on the wild pitch.

The Cubs loaded the bases with nobody out in the eighth but got just one run, on a sacrifice fly by Dexter Fowler. The Cubs did get the tying and lead runs on base in the ninth inning on singles by Anthony Rizzo and Tommy La Stella, but David Ross grounded out to end the game.

Oh, and that Phillies run? The hit by Herrera? That was off Clayton Richard, who was brought in specifically to throw to the left-handed-hitting Herrera. The Clayton Richard Experiment just wasn't working. Richard isn't a LOOGY ("Left-Handed One-Out Guy"), and he was pretty bad all year. Calls from the masses to get rid of Richard were beginning to become loud, but the Cubs didn't really have anyone around who could fill that LOOGY role.

The Cubs wrapped play in Philadelphia with an 8–1 win behind solid pitching by John Lackey and home runs from Kris Bryant and Ben Zobrist. On the same day, they found out that five Cubs were leading in All-Star balloting at their positions: Bryant, Zobrist, Anthony Rizzo, Addison Russell, and Dexter Fowler.

Atlanta was the next stop on the trip. The Braves, still bringing up the rear in the NL East at 17–42, had a weird home-road split. They were just 6–23 at home entering this series, but 11–19 on the road, including the split of the rain-shortened series at Wrigley at the end of April.

So this one should have been easy for the Cubs, right?

Wrong, of course—or I wouldn't have asked that question.

Jason Hammel, who'd come into the game with a 2.09 ERA, faced Bud Norris, a journeyman who'd been yanked out of the starting rotation after posting an 8.74 ERA in April. He'd made only one start since then.

Well, of course you know where this is going; this one's kind of a Vegas-style sucker bet. Or it was Opposite Day, or something. Norris shut down the Cubs on four hits and one run over seven innings, and Hammel allowed a pair of homers—to a team that had hit only 23 in 59 previous games, by far the lowest total in the major leagues. (The Cubs, by comparison, had tripled that total— 69 homers—coming into that series.)

The 5–1 Atlanta win meant that they led the season series between the teams, two games to one. The Braves came into the game 8–27 against teams outside their division, and the Cubs were the first non-NL East team the Braves had defeated more than once in 2016.

Could have made some money on that one in a legal sports book, that's for sure.

The rest of the series played more true to the form of the team with the best record in baseball playing the team with the worst. Saturday's affair featured four Cubs home runs, three off poor Matt Wisler, who didn't make it out of the fourth inning. Jason Heyward, Anthony Rizzo, and Miguel Montero went deep off Wisler, and Kris Bryant added one off Eric O'Flaherty in the fifth in an 8–2 blowout. Three of those batters are left-handed. At the time, the Braves had five home runs by left-handed batters—all season.

The Cubs poured it on even more in the series finale. Only one home run (Javier Baez) was hit, but the Cubs had 15 other hits in a 13–2 blowout that got a bit sloppy afield (four errors), making the only run off Jon Lester in seven innings unearned. The Cubs and Braves would still have one game remaining in their season series, from the April 30 rainout that would be made up at Wrigley Field July 7, but they were certainly happy to say good-bye forever to Turner Field, where they were 30–43 all time, many of those years matching awful Cubs teams against Braves playoff contenders, a situation reversed in 2016. The Braves are moving to the Atlanta suburbs in 2017, into a ballpark the locals say might be hampered by impossible traffic jams and parking nightmares. But at least it won't be a house of horrors for the Cubs.

Then it was on to Washington and a three-game series against a team they'd swept in May at Wrigley Field.

This one would not be nearly as easy as the Wrigley series. In the first game, the Cubs could do absolutely nothing with Max Scherzer, who struck out nine of the first 10 Cubs he faced (a groundout by Ben Zobrist the only exception). Scherzer eventually set down the first 16 Cubs before Addison Russell homered with one out in the sixth. Russell worked Scherzer for a nine-pitch at bat and fouled off several pitches before he hit his laser beam of a home run.

The homer tied the game, 1–1. The tie lasted less than five minutes. Wilson Ramos scorched a ball to right field that Jason Heyward had in his glove before it popped out and over the wall for a home run. The Cubs managed just one other hit off Scherzer, a double by Anthony Rizzo. Scherzer and two Nats relievers struck out 16 Cubs, and the Cubs fell, 4–1.

The next day provided a new Cubs hero when Albert Almora Jr. entered the game in an eighth-inning double switch. The Cubs had blown a 3–1 lead, and the game went to the ninth tied. Almora, playing in just his eighth big-league game, doubled in Addison Russell (who had drawn a leadoff walk) for the game-winner.

The final game in Washington delayed dinner at our house. It began at an odd time for a getaway-day game, 4:05 Eastern time, and didn't end until four hours and 17 minutes later, when Trevor Cahill and Adam Warren couldn't hold a 12th-inning lead, and Jayson Werth singled in the game-winner off Warren.

Before that, Anthony Rizzo had hit a two-run homer in the ninth inning to give the Cubs a 3–2 lead after Stephen Drew hit a pinch-homer off Pedro Strop in the eighth to break a 1–1 tie that had stood since the first inning.

Yes, Stephen Drew, who hadn't played much before this game, but who, coming into the game, had already hit two pinch homers in 2016. Pitch him more carefully, perhaps?

Travis Wood and Cahill had gotten out of a jam in the 11th and Addison Russell singled in the lead run in the top of the 12th, but they couldn't hold it. In the end, this game felt more important than it probably was in the grand scheme of things. If this had been a playoff game between these two clubs, it would have been an instant classic. Instead, it's just another regular-season loss that was likely shaken off by the Cubs by the time they landed at O'Hare late that evening, with little rest before beginning a homestand against the Pirates. They finished regular-season competition with the Nats with a 5–2 advantage, and with the knowledge that they very well might see this bunch again in October, although the Dodgers took care of that possibility in their division series.

The Pirates, along with the Reds, had been one the Cubs' favorite opponents thus far. They'd taken five of the first six, and this series was no different. Jake Arrieta struck out 11 in six shutout innings on Friday and the pen completed a 6–0 shutout, which they had won two pitches into the game. Dexter Fowler singled on Francisco Liriano's first pitch and Matt Szczur put Liriano's second pitch into the bleachers. The six-run blowout increased the Cubs' scoring margin over the Bucs to 44–13 in the seven games between the two clubs. This game was played in glorious weather conditions, temperatures in the low 70s with a light breeze wafting off Lake Michigan, the kind of early-summer afternoon everyone in Chicago waits for while Mother Nature takes her sweet time unveiling good weather while freezing us to death most of April and May, the kind of day you wish you could bottle up and let out in January when Chicagoans need it most.

The Cubs could have scored even more runs that day, as they left 14 runners on base. The game was notable for the major-league debut of Willson Contreras, who took Miguel Montero's place behind the plate for the ninth. He got a welcome to the big leagues you rarely see: a handshake from plate umpire Gary Cederstrom and a pat on the back from the Pirates' Andrew McCutchen, a kind gesture that will surely be remembered.

The Cubs had to come from behind to win Saturday's game, as Jon Lester put them into a 3–1 hole by the fourth inning. David Ross got one of the runs back on a perfectly executed squeeze bunt, and a solo homer from Kris Bryant tied the contest. Bryant's blast landed on the north side of Waveland, a 460-foot blast caught by Ballhawk Dave. Then Ross homered in the sixth to put the Cubs ahead, and Pedro Strop, Travis Wood, and Hector Rondon shut the Pirates down for the seventh Cubs win in the eight games played.

One thing happened in this game that didn't seem significant at the time. Dexter Fowler departed after the first inning with what was later described as "right hamstring discomfort." Joe Maddon didn't seem concerned, saying Fowler's hammy was just "a little sore" and that he'd have an MRI.

Two days later Fowler hit the disabled list. This would turn out to be important, perhaps even more so than the previous injuries to Schwarber and Soler.

Back to the ballpark, it was the Sunday game, ESPN's featured evening contest, that brought perhaps the loudest cheers to date of this remarkable season.

The Cubs homered three times off top Pirates rookie Jameson Taillon in the first three innings (Javier Baez, Kris Bryant, and Anthony Rizzo). Kyle Hendricks allowed a solo shot to Josh Harrison that made it 4–1 Cubs in the fourth, but that was the only run he allowed in six strong innings in which he struck out 12. I never fail to marvel at Hendricks striking out that many while barely touching 90 miles per hour with his fastball. It's a devastating Hendricks changeup that major-league hitters flail away at, and it was working perfectly on that night.

But Hendricks had thrown 100 pitches through six innings, and Joe Maddon, who spent much of the regular season trying to pace his starters, felt that was enough. Up stepped Contreras to pinch-hit. This was his first big-league at bat after his one inning behind the plate Friday.

The crowd had barely sat down from giving Contreras an ovation for just having his name announced as a pinch-hitter when everyone had to stand up and roar again.

Contreras slammed A.J. Schugel's first pitch into the right-center field bleachers. He became the eighth Cub to homer in his first major-league at bat, but just the fourth to do it at Wrigley

Field, and first at Wrigley since Carmelo Martinez inaugurated his MLB career with a Wrigley homer in his first at bat August 22, 1983. (Martinez currently works in the Cubs' baseball operations department as Latin America field coordinator.) He became the first Cub to accomplish this feat since Jorge Soler did it against the Cardinals August 27, 2014, and just the second Cub to homer on his first big-league pitch (the other: pitcher Jim Bullinger, who did it in St. Louis June 8, 1992).

And after Contreras thrilled the Wrigley crowd with this blast? Why he went down to the bullpen and helped warm up Cubs relievers.

Those relievers, incidentally, didn't do a great job on this night. The Cubs took a 6–1 lead into the seventh, but Clayton Richard and Adam Warren got hit hard, and it was 6–4 going into the eighth. The Cubs tacked on four more in that inning, and the 10–4 lead seemed safe, but the Pirates scored a run in the ninth and had two runners on base when Pedro Strop struck out Josh Harrison to end it.

It was likely this game that began to convince Theo & Co. that they had to go out and get some help for the back end of the bullpen for the . . . well, not really the "pennant race," as the Cubs had a 12 ½-game lead on the Cardinals after winning this game, but to line up a good seventh-eighth-ninth inning combination for the postseason. That seemed to be what the cool kids were doing; the Royals had won the World Series in 2015 in part with a bullpen like this.

The win made the Cubs a season-high 27 games over .500 at 47–20. They'd put together ridiculous numbers like this:

- 43–3 when scoring four or more runs
- 37–1 when scoring five or more runs
- 33–0 when scoring six or more runs
- 25 of their wins had been by five or more runs—more than they had losses

The .701 winning percentage after this game, 41 percent of the season done, would produce 114 wins in a full season. They were 25–8 at home, a pace for 61 home wins, which would have shattered the franchise record. Yes, people were actually talking about this. And at the time, they were actually underperforming their Pythagorean projection by four games (in other words, they should have been 51–16 based on their runs scored/allowed totals).

And then the wheels fell off.

The first game against the Cardinals at Wrigley didn't feel so bad. After all, the Cardinals have always been a tough opponent, and the Cubs lost in part because of aggressive baserunning, something Joe Maddon always preaches.

Albert Almora, starting in Fowler's stead, had doubled with one out in the ninth. With Chris Coghlan at the plate, a pitch from Trevor Rosenthal bounced in front of the plate, and Almora, playing in just his 12th big-league game, tried to take third.

This isn't a good idea against Yadier Molina. The pitch didn't get far enough away from Yadi, and he threw Almora out. The crowd groaned, partly because it took a Cubs runner out of scoring position and partly because Cubs fans groan about pretty much everything Molina does.

Coghlan was eventually hit by a Rosenthal pitch, and Ben Zobrist, naturally, singled. That would have scored Almora and tied the game. More groans, even though Coghlan was now at third with two out.

Jason Heyward, who had been struggling at the plate most of the year, popped up to end the game.

One loss! How bad could that be?

Bad, when another similar loss to the Cardinals followed the next night. The Cubs spotted St. Louis a 4–1 lead on a couple of home runs off Jason Hammel. RBI hits by Jason Heyward and Albert Almora Jr. brought the Cubs back to within 4–3 by the fourth.

But there it stayed. The Cubs got runners in scoring position in the seventh and ninth but could not bring anyone home. Frustratingly, they went 0-for-9 with RISP, something the 2015 Cubs struggled with, but so far this year that had not been a problem for the Cubs.

Worst of all, this brought the team's record to 47–22. You know, exactly the record I described in Chapter Three, the "Lou Boudreau Record" of 1977, when they could "kiss the .500 mark goodbye!" but wound up smooching that 81–81 record on the last day of the season.

This team was so much better, so much deeper, than the bunch from 39 years earlier. (Coincidence? That's exactly the length of the Cubs' postseason drought from 1945 to 1984. Cue the eerie Twilight Zone music.) It couldn't happen again.

Could it?

The next game wasn't close. Was that better, not frustratingly losing by one run? Or was having Justin Grimm have a four-run blowup in the sixth inning better, putting the game out of reach? This after Jake Arrieta walked four and threw an alarmingly high number of pitches, 109, without finishing that sixth inning.

(Death is not an option there, incidentally.)

The 7–2 loss provided the Cardinals' first sweep of the Cubs at Wrigley Field since 1988. Worse, Miguel Montero appeared to hurt a knee in an awkward tag try at the plate attempting to tag Yadier Molina on a contact play in that disastrous sixth inning.

It couldn't have been worse, especially being swept by the Cubs' arch-rivals in front of three full houses at Wrigley. Still, in 70 games, the Cubs had lost three straight exactly twice and still led the NL Central by 9 1/2 games.

There couldn't have been a bigger contrast between the rivalry games the Cubs had just finished at their century-old park and the four-game series they were about to begin in the antiseptic, retractable-roofed Marlins Park.

And loss number four in a row, the first four-game losing streak of 2016, was almost tougher to take than losing to the Cardinals.

Jon Lester allowed a pair of solo homers, no shame in one of them: Giancarlo Stanton hit a monstrous blast in the fourth inning and Marcell Ozuna another one in the sixth.

But the Cubs, trailing 2–1, tied the game on a David Ross homer, his eighth. It was the first time in Ross's career he had hit a home run to tie a game in the eighth inning or later, another significant milestone in Ross's farewell tour to baseball, which was turning out statistically to be a far better season than his first with the Cubs in 2015.

Pedro Strop, who had allowed just two runs in his previous 15 appearances (14 innings, 1.29 ERA, 22 strikeouts), was sent in to keep the game tied. Unfortunately, we got "bad Pedro" that night. With two out and a runner on first, Strop uncorked a wild pitch, which was followed by an RBI single by Stanton. The next hitter, J.T. Realmuto, hit a sharp grounder in the direction of Javier Baez. He got a glove on it, but it went past him down the left-field line, scoring Stanton and making the score 4–2, where it stayed for the Cubs' fourth straight loss.

Panic? No. Still leading the division by nine games. Nervousness? Of course. What Cubs fan doesn't go through at least part of every baseball season a bit nervous?

The rest of the series in Miami didn't go much better, even though the Cubs ended the season-high four-game losing streak by defeating the Marlins, 5–4, in the second game of the series. This one looked like it'd be easy; four Cubs runs came across in the first inning, three of them on homers by Kris Bryant and Willson Contreras. The Contreras homer gave him three in seven career games. If you think that sounds like a lot, he joined three of his teammates in accomplishing that feat! Jorge Soler, Javier Baez, and Jason Heyward (with the Braves) all socked three homers in their first seven games.

Addison Russell booted the first ball he saw in the bottom of the first, but the next two men were out. That means the inning should have been over, but Kyle Hendricks lost command and walked the bases loaded.

What happened next is the sort of thing that always seemed to happen when the Cubs were going bad: one of their former minor leaguers coming back to bite them. This time it was Justin Bour, someone never really on the prospect radar in the Cubs system. He was picked up by the Marlins in the 2013 Rule 5 draft after five uninspiring years in the Cubs minors.

You know what's coming next even if you didn't see the game, or you're reading about this season for the first time. Bour hit a grand slam off Hendricks, tying the game. It turned out to be the only hit Hendricks allowed in five innings, and the Cubs eventually pushed across the winning run on a Contreras single in the seventh, providing these odd statistical notes:

- It was the first time in Cubs history that they allowed a first-inning grand slam and no other runs in the rest of the game.
- It was the first time the Cubs had won a game after allowing a first-inning slam in 42 years, since June 28, 1974, at Montreal.
- Hendricks became the first Cubs pitcher since 1913 (the "Baseball-Reference.com era") to have a start of at least five innings and allow four or more runs on only one hit.

But a win's a win, and the plus-163 run differential the Cubs had after this game (their 72nd of the year) was similar to those of dominant pennant-winning teams like the 1912 Giants, the 1927 Yankees, the 1929 Athletics (who beat the Cubs in the World Series!), and the 1936–37 and 1939 Yankees.

So not to worry, right?

Worry lined the face of the Cubs fan after they dropped the final two games of the series in Miami, a 9–6 beating of John Lackey (seven runs in fewer than five innings on Saturday) and a 6–1 loss Sunday in which Jose Fernandez would dominate with 13 strikeouts and the Marlins would push across runs in the late innings in part helped by some favorable replay reviews.

During this weekend, the news came out that former Cubs outfielder Jim Hickman, known as "Gentleman Jim" for his kindly manner, had passed away in his home in Tennessee at age 79. Hickman, part of the star-crossed 1969 team, had his best year for the Cubs in 1970 when he hit 32 home runs and drove in 115 and made the All-Star team. If you're familiar with the video of Pete Rose crashing into Ray Fosse at the plate for the winning run in that year's All-Star Game, it was Hickman's single that drove Rose in.

Ron Santo gone, Ernie Banks gone, now Hickman. And Billy Williams and Fergie Jenkins, both now in their 70s. They couldn't bring it home for the Cubs, but I wanted so badly to see at least some of my childhood heroes see the Cubs win the World Series.

Even with the series loss in Miami, the Cubs still led the Central by nine games.

And they'd have more fun in three games in Cincinnati than most teams would have in an entire season.

Any chance of Jake Arrieta throwing another no-hitter against the Reds vanished in the first inning of the first game of the set, after a pair of walks and a double scored two runs for the home team.

But this only tied the game, as Kris Bryant had doubled in a run and eventually scored on a sacrifice fly in the top of the inning.

That was just the beginning of what became known as "The Kris Bryant Game." Bryant set a franchise record with 16 total bases on three home runs and two doubles. Read that sequence of hits carefully again: three home runs and two doubles.

Bryant became the first player in major-league history to ever do that in one game, and the first Cub to have five extra-base hits in a game since 1885. Just so you know that's not a typo, that's "Eighteen Eighty-Five," 131 years ago. It was just about then that people really started to take notice of the Cubs' second-year third baseman and to murmur "MVP." He became the youngest Cub (by 10 days, over Ernie Banks) to hit three homers in a game.

And it almost wasn't enough, because Jake again wasn't sharp. He allowed only four hits in five innings, but walked four and threw 93 pitches, and had to be lifted. The Reds nibbled away at the Cubs' bullpen until it was 8–7 Cubs after seven innings, too close for comfort. Bryant's third homer, in the eighth, followed immediately by one from Anthony Rizzo, brought the margin to 10–8, and the Cubs tacked on one more in the ninth for an 11–8 win, breaking another baby losing streak at two.

The next night involved more bullpen meltdown. Hector Rondon was called on to make a multi-inning save after Billy Hamilton homered off Jon Lester to make the score 2–1 Cubs in the eighth. Hector got out of that one but hit a batter and gave up a single in the ninth, and with two out, Eugenio Suarez tied the game.

That led to a protracted tussle of nothing. No one did much of anything in the 10th, 11th, or 12th innings. In the 13th, with the Cubs out of position players and Joel Peralta replacing Trevor Cahill, out ran Travis Wood to left field. Wood had been an outfielder in high school, and Maddon revealed after the season that he had watched how seriously Wood took shagging flies during batting practice, and he and Wood had discussed just such a scenario that might happen during the season.

Wood became the first Cubs pitcher to play the outfield since Sean Marshall, who'd done it for one batter in 2009. Irony: Wood was acquired in a trade for Marshall, the first deal that Theo Epstein and his management team made in late 2011.

Wood was the first of three Cubs hurlers to play a position other than pitcher in this one. Wood and Spencer Patton swapped places between mound and outfield a couple of times. Eventually, Pedro Strop completed the game in left field, looking for all the world as if he actually wanted someone to hit the ball to him.

Before Strop could take the field as an outfielder, though, the Cubs had taken a big lead. A walk and two singles plated the lead run. An intentional walk to Anthony Rizzo loaded the bases, and Jason Hammel, yet another fish-out-of-water pitcher, was sent up to pinch-hit for Patton. Hammel's not a bad hitter, so this wasn't automatic-out territory, but he hit into a force play at the plate.

With two out, Javier Baez was the next hitter. He launched one deep into the Cincinnati night for a grand slam and a 7–2 lead, and another bit of Cubs lore was created: the 15th-inning slam was the latest inning-wise in franchise history.

Quite a bit of that "something since never in franchise history" going around this year.

The Cubs completed the three-game sweep in an afternoon crushing of the Reds June 29. They hit three homers (Anthony Rizzo, Addison Russell, Albert Almora) off Reds rookie Cody Reed, and Kyle Hendricks put together another solid outing in the ballpark where he'd made his major-league debut just about two years earlier.

The 9–2 win was the ninth in ten games against the Reds thus far in 2016. They'd outscored the Reds, 87–32, and taking out the 13–5 loss, the margin of victory in the nine wins was 82–19.

Eleven games ahead. Back to 25 games over .500. Ship righted, right?

Uh . . . not quite. There was still one day left in June, but since the Cubs finished that month with a 16–12 record, I'm going to let that June 30 game in New York spill over to July, where it belonged.

Chapter 7

July: Righting the Ship

If the Cubs thought July was going to begin any better than June ended, they were mistaken.

The Cubs/Mets game from June 30 goes in July's chapter because it was part of an error-filled, bullpen-meltdown, disastrous four-game sweep at Citi Field, making six straight games the Cubs had lost there dating back to the 2015 NLCS.

Details? Well, I'll be a little judicious about these because they're not pretty. A 3–0 lead in the first game vanished with some poor bullpen work from Joel Peralta, who really was only on this team due to his history with Joe Maddon. At age 40, and two years removed from his last year pitching for Maddon with the Rays, Peralta's velocity was down, and thus, when he threw strikes, they got hit. In the seventh, Brandon Nimmo, a rookie playing in his fifth major-league game, found a Peralta pitch to his liking and singled to make the score 3–2 Cubs. Pedro Strop replaced Peralta, and Neil Walked doubled. The tying run scored, and then the eventual winning run crossed the plate on a wild throw by Javier Baez.

The next night was a nightmare for Jason Hammel. After Hammel had pitched so well most of the first half, the Mets hit five home runs off him in just four innings, a Citi Field record for them that also tied their franchise record. He became just the sixth pitcher in Cubs history to allow five home runs in a single game, and you probably don't want to know who the others are, as it's an ugly list. (If you must know: Travis Wood in 2012, Carlos Zambrano in 2011, Ismael Valdez in 2000, Steve Stone in 1974, and Warren Hacker in 1954. The Cubs actually won the Valdez game, 6–5. The Cubs lost this one, 10–2.)

The third game of the series was almost a repeat of the first. This time, the Cubs came from behind to tie the game, 2–2, on a single by Kris Bryant and a majestic home run from Anthony Rizzo in the fourth, but Jake Arrieta continued his worrisome trend of throwing way too many pitches, 108 in just 5 1/3 innings. He also gave up eight hits, including a two-run homer by Neil Walker. Ben Zobrist homered to bring the Cubs to within one, but they could not do anything against the Mets' bullpen tandem of Addison Reed and Jeurys Familia and lost again, 4–3.

Remember the Mets home run record I mentioned two paragraphs ago? Two days after setting it, the Mets tied it by again smacking five home runs, though this time they spread the power around, hitting them off three Cubs pitchers (Jon Lester, Spencer Patton, and Joel Peralta) instead of just one. Wilmer Flores went 6-for-6, the first player to have six hits in a game against the Cubs since Freddy Sanchez of the Pirates in 2009. Only a few weeks after Lester had the worst game of his Cubs career, this one was the worst of his career, period: nine hits and eight earned runs in 1 1/3 innings, 56 pitches thrown to record four outs.

It got so bad that Joe Maddon decided to rest his weary bullpen and let Miguel Montero pitch the eighth inning of this 14–3, football-score disaster. Montero wound up being the only Cubs "pitcher" not to allow a home run that afternoon. It created a bit of humor for everyone, including Mets beat writer Anthony DiComo, who tweeted: "Miguel Montero is throwing 79–81 mph. The scoreboard is calling them splitters and changeups. I don't, um, think that's the case."

The Cubs limped back to Wrigley Field with a 4–7 road trip but still eight games in front in the NL Central, due to the great start that had now turned into an ugly stretch of 10 losses in 14 games. What had happened?

One of the factors was the injury to Dexter Fowler suffered in the final game of the Pittsburgh series. At first not viewed as significant, it kept Fowler out for nearly a month. He missed 28 games, during which the Cubs went 11–17. Missing Fowler's "You go, we go" bat at the top of the lineup wasn't the only reason for those losses, but it was certainly one of the biggest factors.

Dex was still out of the lineup when the Cubs came home for a brief four-game homestand. That was another factor in the Cubs' midseason slump: playing 24 games without an off day due to the April 30 rainout with the Braves being rescheduled for July 7, and around that time also playing 14 of 17 on the road. That'll do a number on even the best team.

The Cubs did turn it around—for one day, a brilliantly sunny Fourth of July on which the team unfurled a ginormous American flag that covered the entire outfield. I saw this flag when it was wrapped up and placed (with a cover beneath it, of course) on the lower bleacher concourse beneath right field. It literally took up the entire length of the concourse.

The Cubs unfurled quite a number of hits against the Reds, their favorite 2015 punching bag and the club they had just swept in Cincinnati the previous week, on this holiday. A 12-hit attack featured three "bombs bursting in air," home runs from Kris Bryant, Willson Contreras, and Addison Russell, and the Cubs won, 10–4. Kyle Hendricks again did not allow an earned run at home (just one unearned tally), and the four-game losing streak was over.

Unfortunately, another losing stretch was about to begin, and this time, it would extend to five games. Fortunately, that turned out to be the season's longest, but it was not fun and it was mostly due to pitching failures, both from the bullpen and the starting rotation. Dropping five straight to the awful Reds (twice), horrid Braves (once), and sort-of-contending Pirates (twice), the Cubs were outscored, 38–21, and looked bad in pretty much all phases of the game.

Oh, you want to read about some of these losses? I was going to ignore them and head straight to the All-Star break, but a few details should suffice.

The first loss to the Reds was so weird that I used the Internet Shrug (¯_(ツ)_/¯) as the headline. Plate umpire Jerry Meals missed so many calls that Joe Maddon finally had enough and got himself tossed for arguing them. That wasn't the reason the Cubs lost that game, 9–5, though; they lost because after bringing the game to within 6–5 in the sixth, Javier Baez decided (on his own, apparently) to bunt with two runners on base. He popped the bunt up, and the Cubs didn't score—and then there was more bullpen failure, including a two-run homer served up to Jay Bruce by Pedro Strop in the ninth.

This might have been another sign to the front office that they needed bullpen help. Joel Peralta threw a scoreless inning in that loss. That got him designated for assignment the next day, when the Cubs recalled Adam Warren from Triple-A Iowa. Warren had been sent down to stretch him out to start against the Reds, since the Cubs were going through that stretch of 24 consecutive games without an off day, and Joe and the brass wanted to give everyone in the rotation a break.

Warren did great. He threw 93 pitches in five innings, allowing just three hits and one run (a solo homer), and departed with a 3–1 lead.

Trevor Cahill came in and did fine in the sixth but allowed a pair of singles and then a disastrous three-run homer to Tucker Barnhart. Carl Edwards Jr. wild-pitched a run in, and the Cubs had lost a series to the Reds for the first time since August 2015.

And then it was time for the makeup game against the Braves on Thursday, July 7.

A miserable, cold, all-day rain had forced this postponement. And guess what. It rained again before this one started, heavy at times, not ending until just about the originally scheduled game time of 7:05.

Not long after that, someone fell (or jumped, it wasn't clear) out of the right-field bleachers and lay flat on his back for a long time on the warning track. Eventually, he was carted off the field on a stretcher and taken to a local hospital. I heard later that this man got up and walked out of the hospital under his own power the next day. He was very, very lucky, and having said that, this was a remarkably stupid thing to do. The Wrigley Field bleacher wall is nearly 12 feet high. Many years ago, probably in the late 1990s, I saw someone else do something similar to this; that man landed on his feet and broke both his ankles. Please, please, please: if you are ever in the bleachers at Wrigley, *don't do that.* Just don't.

Don't do what the Cubs did that night, either: lose to a team that came into Wrigley 24 1/2 games worse than they were. Yes, I know, on any given night but really, this one was pretty ugly. Jason Hammel allowed a two-run homer to Nick Markakis in the first inning. Then the bullpen did a decent job of holding the Braves down (including Kyle Hendricks's first big-league relief appearance) until the Cubs could come back with a three-run rally in the eighth, with RBI hits from Anthony Rizzo and Willson Contreras.

Then Hector Rondon entered in to close, but he didn't. Markakis hit a 3–2 two-seamer into the bleachers to tie the game. By this time, Kris Bryant had been removed after being hit twice by pitches ("a little banged up," said Joe Maddon later), and it would have been nice to have him around when the game went into extra innings.

Before that, though, there was a bit of extracurricular activity when a Rondon pitch got too inside for Jeff Francoeur's liking. That pitch was inside, but not remarkably so. Benches and bullpens cleared, but all that happened was some milling around. When order was restored, Francoeur walked and then stole second, his first steal of the year and first since 2013.

Spencer Patton issued a leadoff walk in the 11th. You know how those can come back to bite you, and bitten Patton was, by a pair of singles scoring a run. The Cubs had a pair of singles in the bottom of the inning, but Addison Russell quashed that rally by hitting into a double play, and there were maybe 5,000 remaining out of a full house when Jeimer Candelario popped into short center field at 12:34 a.m. to end it.

Candelario, considered part of the Cubs' future, was shipped back to Iowa after that loss. He never did return, even as a September call-up.

Then it was on to Pittsburgh, where the Cubs had swept the Bucs in May, for a three-game set leading into the All-Star break. Surely this would break the losing spell.

You're expecting a "Stop calling me Shirley" line here, right? Maybe a showing of the movie Airplane! would have broken some of the tension around the Cubs and us as fans right about then, because the beginning of the series in Pittsburgh just made things worse.

Jake Arrieta started the first game of the series and put the Cubs in a hole early when David Freese (solo homer) and Sean Rodriguez, the Gatorade-puncher from the 2015 wild-card game, hit a two-run shot. Trailing, 3–1, in the sixth, Miguel Montero tied the game with a two-run blast of his own. Anthony Rizzo gave the Cubs the lead with a solo homer in the seventh.

Joe left Jake out there for the seventh, and he got himself in trouble with a walk and two singles. Even though Jake was at only 88 pitches, Joe brought in Travis Wood. A throwing error, a single, and a groundout plated four runs, and the Cubs lost the game.

I mean, how do you explain numbers like this for Jake?

> First nine starts: 1.29 ERA, 63.0 IP, 2 HR, .153 Opponents BA, 0.841 WHIP

> Last nine starts: 4.38 ERA, 51.1 IP, 5 HR, .243 Opponents BA, 1.402 WHIP

The first nine starts, he was Cy Young Jake from 2015. The next nine starts, he was Ricky Nolasco. (No offense to Nolasco, but he was a worse-than-average starter on the worst team in baseball in 2016.)

It got worse the next day, and I'll spare you the carnage, except to say that Cubs pitchers allowed four home runs in a 12–6 loss that didn't feel that close. It was the Cubs' fifth straight loss, a season high, and meant they were now 5–15 since that 47–20 start, by far the worst record in baseball over that three-week span.

How does a team go from being historically good to being in 1962 Mets territory in three weeks? Only part of it could be explained by the absence of Dexter Fowler at the top of the lineup; both starting and relief pitching had really bad days through this span. The Cubs were outscored, 123–90, over those 20 games, and several blowouts made it all feel much worse than it was.

I knew this team was good, too good to be this bad. I tried to put down the nagging feelings that this swoon would get worse and spiral into a collapse. I kept thinking Joe Maddon and the player-leaders like Anthony Rizzo and David Ross wouldn't let that happen.

That's why the next day's game felt so good, even though it was a bit of a struggle to beat the Pirates, 6–5, in the last game before the All-Star break. Even this one went back and forth; just like the previous day, the Cubs went out to a 2–0 lead, blew it, took another lead at 5–4, blew that one, and finally scored the eventual winning run on a single by Kris Bryant in the eighth.

Anthony Rizzo was helping lead this charge by being on one of his patented hot streaks. He had his second straight four-hit game, and in a hitting streak that reached nine games entering the break, he went 16-for-36 (.444) with four doubles, a triple, two home runs, and eight runs scored. At one point over the last two games before the break, he had hits in eight consecutive at bats.

When Hector Rondon got John Jaso to ground to second to end the game, it was a sigh of relief for everyone, including the players, six of whom would head to San Diego for All-Star festivities.

So the All-Star break wasn't really a break for Anthony Rizzo, Ben Zobrist, Addison Russell, Kris Bryant, or Jon Lester, all of whom played in the All-Star Game. (Dexter Fowler was not quite back from his injury, but went to be honored for being elected, and Jake Arrieta did not appear.) It was the first time an entire infield had started the game since 1963, when four Cardinals did. And Bryant made the most of his evening by homering off the White Sox' Chris Sale in the first inning. It wasn't enough, even though half the Cubs' offense was there, to prevent an American League win, meaning that if the Cubs got to the World Series, they'd have to open on the road, even if they had the best record in baseball.

Let me interrupt here to say that Bud Selig's "This Time It Counts" is the dumbest idea of baseball's twenty-first century. The All-Star Game is an exhibition, played for fun, not played the same way regular-season or postseason games are played, and Bud's idea was an extreme overreaction to the All-Star Game tie in his native Milwaukee in 2002, due to both sides running out of pitchers.

There were other ways to fix this, but Bud chose the worst possible one. A few years later, he blamed this on hotel-room availability. No, I am not making that up, he actually told reporters in 2007 that if they didn't know where the World Series would begin four months ahead of time, they might not get enough hotel rooms, never mind that this only cut the possible number of host cities in half, and the NBA and NHL seem to be able to accomplish this task on short notice every year.

The Cubs should have had Game 1 of the World Series at Wrigley Field because they won more games during the season than anyone else. It's just that simple.

Interlude

People ask me all the time why I get to Wrigley Field so early, in some cases hours before the gates open.

Wrigley Field's bleachers are unreserved seating, among the last such seats anywhere in baseball. They've been so ever since the famed brick-and-ivy stands were first built in 1937, and that's continued through two reconstructions (2006 and 2015). It makes for community; people choose their own seats, and many of us who are season-ticket holders have seating areas we have gravitated to and like to sit in. Season-ticket holders are permitted early entry into the bleachers primarily for this purpose, so they can choose their own seats ahead of single-game ticket holders. It also helps if you want friends who can only come a few times a year to join you; with unreserved seating you can hold seats next to you for them, at least until game time. Sometimes we have only three or four people in our group, but for big games (Cardinals, say), we can have as many as 20. Other groups of bleacher season-ticket holders in other parts of the bleachers do the same thing. I've been a bleacher regular since the late 1970s and a season-ticket holder since 1993, the first year the Cubs offered a bleacher season ticket.

Another reason Miriam and I enjoy coming to the bleacher line early is to watch the neighborhood awaken from its quiet state into the bustling area accommodating more than 40,000 baseball fans, something you might not think a city neighborhood can handle, but all those people almost seamlessly weave themselves in as game time approaches.

It's also a social time for us; since many of our season-ticket holder friends choose seats in other parts of the bleachers, it's a good time for us to socialize with them, an important part of being part of a community that goes back nearly 80 years. Of course, none of those original bleacherites are still around, but there's a connection through some older fans to bleacher fans from the 1960s "Bleacher Bums" era, or even before. People who arrive early—though not quite as early as we do—can leave their backpacks for us to watch while they head to Starbucks or Murphy's or just walk around the neighborhood.

Then there are the stupid questions we sometimes get asked while waiting in line. I swear this is true—while waiting in line, at the bleacher gate, wearing Cubs gear, we have been asked more than once: "Is there a game today?"

We've thought of answers like, "No, we just like sitting here," but have never broken that out. Instead, we just politely answer, "Yes," and the questioner moves on, not knowing we've been laughing at them.

Since the Cubs reinstalled the brick pavers that people paid for a decade or so ago, commemorating family members or other Cubs fans important in their lives, we often see folks looking for their bricks (they learn the location, which are all in various areas where there's a larger brick with a famous name from Cubs history, from Fan Services). It's odd to see someone slowly approach the front of the line looking down, then we realize what they're doing. Occasionally a backpack has to be moved to let those folks access their bricks and take photos.

Sometimes some of the ballhawks from the corner of Waveland and Kenmore will stop by and say hello. They're always the ones who find out first if Joe Maddon's team is having batting practice.

Occasionally, a Cubs player or coach will walk by on his way to work. We often see pitching coach Chris Bosio pass by the line— but he's always got earbuds in, presumably listening to music, so the most we get is a nod of acknowledgment. Cubs gameday employees, concession workers, Walter the scorecard vendor, and others we know, pass by on their way to work and greet us. Sometimes we arrive before the Cubs facilities workers come out to set up the barricades and magnetometers, so we can watch that happen. There's a private vendor who's rented out space behind 3701 N. Kenmore to sell Cubs merchandise, and we watch them set up. One day a food delivery truck tried to back into the alley next to that building and didn't realize how low the electrical cables were hanging and accidentally disconnected one of them, cutting off electric power to a few buildings in the area.

We watched, one crowded day, a nonlocal fire truck try to negotiate a crush of people on Waveland and bend the stop sign at the Sheffield corner. The fire truck and ambulance from Engine 78 across from Gate K usually make several runs before the gates open and more once the game starts (you've probably heard the sirens on the TV broadcasts). One afternoon before a postseason game, an older woman slipped and fell on the Waveland sidewalk. A friend of mine offered to run down to the fire station to get the paramedics to help her.

Before some day games, we have had enough people so a trip to Dunkin' Donuts on Addison would be made and a dozen donuts brought back for early arrivals. One early Saturday morning, we had enough people to play a spirited game of Uno. Or we just discuss our lives, or dissect the previous day's game and share and discuss who's in the lineup for that afternoon or evening. This is a place where we've made lifelong friends, a community that's been created from a common interest—the Cubs—but it's become much more than that. It's more like family.

So it's more than just "waiting in line." It's a social occasion, it's immersing ourselves in the world of baseball around Wrigley Field for an entire day, or evening. I wouldn't have it any other way.

The second half of the 2016 season beckons. Let's get back to the action!

***

Rest gotten, at least for most of the squad, the Cubs and their fans reassembled at Wrigley Field for the second half on July 15, to begin a three-game series against the Texas Rangers.

If you had told me at the end of spring training that the Cubs would begin this game 18 games over .500 and with a seven-game lead in the NL Central, I'd have been ecstatic.

Instead, it was nervous time, because the Cubs had been 27 games over .500 just three weeks earlier and had had a lead as large as 12 1/2 games. So while the lead was still comfortable and the winning percentage put the team on pace for 98 wins, I wanted to see them start playing as they had for most of the first half.

And they did so, right away. A 6–0 win over the Rangers to kick off the second half featured six shutout innings from Kyle Hendricks, spectacular defense by Javier Baez, Anthony Rizzo, Kris Bryant, and Albert Almora Jr., and a five-run sixth inning that put the game away, with Addison Russell and Matt Szczur contributing key singles.

For me, a big fan of Hendricks ever since he was acquired, it was gratifying to see him start a run like this. Through this game he had an 0.87 ERA over his last six appearances (five starts) covering 31 innings, and in that time he'd allowed 23 hits and 10 walks, and struck out 28, this from a guy who doesn't break 90 on the Wrigley pitch speed meter. It became a site meme at Bleed Cubbie Blue: "All he does is get guys out."

The next day didn't figure to be easy, with Rangers ace Yu Darvish scheduled to start. Darvish had missed most of two years after Tommy John surgery and had made three starts after coming back before going back on the disabled list. This was his first start after returning from that stint, and he was not sharp. He allowed only two hits, but the Cubs worked him for four walks and forced him out of the game in the fifth inning, after he'd thrown 90 pitches.

Jason Hammel threw six solid innings in the 3–1 win, and the Cubs had a three-game winning streak that put them back to 20 games over .500 and eight games in front, and it started to feel like that 5–15 stretch was a bad dream, rather than any sort of season-long reality.

Cole Hamels started the final game of the series for the Rangers, and naturally, the thoughts of Cubs fans went back to the last time he'd appeared in Wrigley, when he no-hit the Cubs for the Phillies. That ended the Cubs' streak of games in which they had not been no-hit at 7,920, a major-league record that had spawned a Twitter account (@CubsNoHitStreak), among other things.

Hamels started this one like he not only wanted to repeat the no-no, but top it. He struck out the first six Cubs he saw. They managed an unearned run in the third on an error followed by a double by Javier Baez, but the Rangers had a 2–0 lead by that time, and Hamels threw eight strong innings, giving up no further runs.

Joe Maddon likes to call series like these, winning two of three, "meatloaf." If that sounds silly, it is, a little, but there's a reason: there was a 1970s rock song titled "Two Out of Three Ain't Bad," recorded by an artist named Meat Loaf. Thus the terminology, and indeed, two out of three in every baseball series you play wouldn't be bad, not at all.

Footnote: We didn't know it at the time, but this game would be the final time Prince Fielder would ever play at Wrigley Field. After slicing through Cubs pitching for years as a Brewer, Fielder signed with the Tigers and was eventually traded to the Rangers, where he missed much of 2014 with injuries, and after bouncing back in 2015, played poorly for much of 2016. He would play just one more game after that Wrigley series, go back on the disabled list and, a few weeks later, announce his retirement after doctors told him he would no longer be cleared to play after his second spinal-fusion surgery.

Then it was time to see the Mets again, and you'll forgive all of us if we weren't real happy to see them after being swept in the

NLCS in 2015 and then losing four straight at Citi Field just a few weeks earlier.

The first game stopped all that nonsense. Jon Lester threw 7⅔ innings of four-hit, one-run ball, and Anthony Rizzo punctuated a 10-pitch at bat against Steven Matz with a home run (his 22nd, and the Cubs' first since the All-Star break). It was good to see Lester throw this well against the Mets after his career-worst outing in New York against them, and Rizzo was one of the hottest hitters in baseball since June 1: .363/.444/.705, 15 doubles, 11 home runs, and 31 RBIs. Javy Baez threw in another one of his highlight-reel defensive plays for good measure.

If you are looking for one final reason why the Cubs intensified their search for late-inning bullpen help, look no further than the July 19 game against the Mets, which went into the ninth inning tied 1–1 after one of Jake Arrieta's better outings of the year: seven innings, five hits, one walk, and one run. The Cubs pushed across an unearned run in the third when Willson Contreras doubled, went to third on a wild pitch, and scored on a throwing error by Mets catcher Rene Rivera.

But Hector Rondon, called on to preserve the tie in the ninth, could not. A two-out single by Rivera gave the Mets a 2–1 lead.

Even then, the Cubs had a chance to come back. The Cubs loaded the bases off Jeurys Familia on a pair of walks and a bunt by Javier Baez that was badly mishandled by Mets third baseman Jose Reyes. The bunt likely would have gone foul if he'd let it, and then Reyes made a bad throw, allowing Baez to reach. Bases loaded, nobody out!

Joe Maddon likes squeeze bunts; Cubs hitters often execute them well.

So why didn't Joe ask Matt Szczur, pinch-hitting for Rondon, to lay down a squeeze? Addison Russell, on third base, is a good baserunner, and Reyes had just misplayed a bunt. Further, until this year Reyes had literally not played a single inning at third base since 2000, when he was a 17-year-old playing in the Appalachian League!

Finally, Reyes was playing back at third base, not expecting a bunt, and Szczur's a pretty good bunter.

I've made a pretty good case for a squeeze here, right?

Well, if Joe thought of it, he didn't do it, because Szczur grounded to James Loney at first. Loney threw home for the force, and Kris Bryant hit into a game-ending double play.

Frustrating.

The Cubs made up for it, partly, by meatloafing the Mets the next afternoon. Kyle Hendricks kept up his amazing run of Wrigley Field pitching by throwing 6⅓ scoreless innings. Anthony Rizzo blasted two homers off Bartolo Colon to pace the 6–2 win.

Just after the game ended, the Cubs front office fired its first salvo into a bullpen that had been shaky for some stretches of the first half. They traded media darling Dan Vogelbach, a minor-leaguer who's not likely to be more than a DH at the big-league level, and minor-league pitcher Paul Blackburn to the Seattle Mariners for lefthander Mike Montgomery.

Montgomery was a No. 1 pick (sandwich round) of the Kansas City Royals in 2008. Four years later, he was swapped to the Tampa Bay Rays in the deal that sent James Shields to Kansas City. That's where Joe Maddon first saw him, but he never played in the majors in Tampa, instead toiling in Triple-A for two years before being swapped to Seattle for Erasmo Ramirez.

The Mariners used him as a starter in 2015, with mixed results. He was moved to the bullpen in Seattle to start 2016 but started a couple of games just before the trade; perhaps Mariners management had done this after learning of trade interest.

It seemed clear that Montgomery was being acquired to bolster the bullpen with the possibility of starting somewhere down the road.

Speaking of the road, it was calling, but just for a Cubs team bus ride to Milwaukee.

I decided to skip heading to Milwaukee for this series to rest up for four straight games against the White Sox. The Cubs, though, did not hesitate to start right up against Milwaukee starter Jimmy

Nelson in the series opener. Dexter Fowler led off the game with a home run, and the Cubs led 4–0 by the end of the second inning. Jason Hammel put together another solid outing for a 5–2 win.

It didn't work out that well the next night. Kyle Davies tied Cubs bats in knots; even so, they were trailing just 3–1 when John Lackey left the game. Unfortunately, the back end of the Cubs bullpen didn't keep the game close. Adam Warren got touched up for a pair of runs, and then it was time for Mike Montgomery's Cubs debut.

Let's just say it could have gone better. Montgomery ran the count to 3–1 on the first batter he faced, Kirk Nieuwenhuis, and then Nieuwenhuis smacked a home run off Montgomery.

Nieuwenhuis, a replacement-level player if ever there were one (92 OPS+, 3.0 bWAR through five seasons), weirdly dominated Cubs pitching in 2016.

Against the Cubs: .333/.472/.762, 14-for-42, 11 walks, three doubles, and five home runs. Against everyone else: .191/.301/.331, 56-for-293, 45 walks, 15 doubles, and eight home runs

I mean, it's like he was the worst player in baseball against everyone except the Cubs, against whom he put up All-Star numbers. The five homers were off Jake Arrieta, John Lackey, Jason Hammel, Hector Rondon, and Montgomery.

Maybe the Cubs should sign him. If you can't beat him, have him join you. Right?

The Cubs won the series Sunday, giving them seven wins in their previous 10 games. They'd let the Brewers run out to a 4–1 lead before exploding for a five-run seventh, highlighted by doubles from Anthony Rizzo and Tommy La Stella.

Joe Nathan, whom the Cubs had signed off the scrap heap, threw a scoreless sixth inning and posted the win in his first game with the Cubs. Nathan's Cubs career lasted just three games, though. But this appearance, in a win, was worthy of mention.

Remember that home run I mentioned that Nieuwenhuis hit off Hector Rondon? It came in the Sunday game, with two out in the ninth, making it a one-run game and perhaps further intensifying the Cubs' search for relief help.

It would come early the next morning in the form of Aroldis Chapman.

The rumors started flying late in the evening of Sunday, July 24, that the Cubs were putting together a package to get the flame-throwing closer from the New York Yankees.

By midmorning Monday, it was a done deal: Adam Warren would be heading back to New York along with three minor leaguers: Billy McKinney (who'd been acquired along with Addison Russell two years earlier), Rashad Crawford, and the Cubs' top prospect, Gleyber Torres.

This is the sort of "win-now" move that teams in the Cubs' position often make. Torres, just 19 years old, could be a star for the Yankees for years to come; Chapman might not even stick with the Cubs beyond 2016.

But the recent bullpen failures made Theo Epstein desire a lockdown closer, and the ability to move Hector Rondon to the eighth inning and Pedro Strop to the seventh. It was with such a trio that the Kansas City Royals won the World Series in 2015.

Chapman did not come without controversy. He had been involved in a domestic violence incident with his girlfriend the previous offseason, though no charges were filed. That incident, in part, was what prompted the Reds to trade him. In fact, at first he appeared headed to the Dodgers before landing in New York.

Justifiably, many female—and male, too—fans were upset with the acquisition. One fan, Caitlin Swieca, declared that she'd donate $10 to a local antidomestic violence organization every time Chapman posted a save for the Cubs. This pledge, sent out via Twitter, prompted dozens of other fans to do the same thing, a good result. Chapman saved 16 games for the Cubs during the regular season and 4 more during the postseason, so everyone won—the Cubs, and organizations devoted to stamping out the scourge of domestic violence.

Chapman joined the team in Chicago—not at Wrigley Field but on the South Side, where the Cubs were beginning a four-game, home-and-home series against the Chicago White Sox.

One of the good things about playing the Sox every year—and honestly, there aren't many as these games are treated like war by White Sox fans, while Cubs fans are somewhat sick of them—is that the Cubs can play two, or sometimes three, road games without leaving town. The 2016 schedule, so road-heavy leading into the All-Star break, was Chicago-centric for the first five weeks of the second half. The Cubs had to get on a plane just once in that span—a three-game, one-series "road trip" to Oakland in early August. The schedule from July 15 through August 18 read like this:

July 15–17: Home vs. Rangers
July 18–20: Home vs. Mets
July 22–24: Bus ride to Milwaukee to face Brewers
July 25–26: At White Sox
July 27–28: Home vs. White Sox
July 29–31: Home vs. Mariners
August 1–3: Home vs. Marlins
August 5–7: At Oakland vs. Athletics
August 9–10: Home vs. Angels
August 11–14: Home vs. Cardinals
August 16–18: Home vs. Brewers

So that's 29 of 32 games played within 90 miles of Chicago. I don't think it's entirely a coincidence that the Cubs went 24–8 in those 32 games. Being at home, in your own bed (in fact, some Cubs might have gone home for an evening or two while the team was in Milwaukee), is much more comfortable than even modern, first-class sports team travel arrangements.

In the series opener at the Cell, Melky Cabrera stole a home run from Kris Bryant. Literally. He reached over the wall in front of the Sox bullpen; the baseball was past the barrier, but he brought

April 11, 2016: One of the most anticipated Opening Days—er, nights—in Cubs history.

Fans fly the "W" flag after the team wins its home opener against the Cincinnati Reds, 5–3. (Photographs courtesy of Sue Skowronski)

Since taking the helm in 2015, the "Mad Scientist," Joe Maddon has quickly turned the franchise around. Not only has be brought the club their first winning record since 2008, but their first 100-win season since 1935. (AP Images)

A beautiful pregame display at Wrigley on May 30, before the Cubs were set to take on the Los Angeles Dodgers. (Sue Skowronski)

Kyle Schwarber's home run ball from the 2015 NLDS, replaced where it landed on top of the right-field video board. (Sue Skowronski)

In the third game of the season, on April 7, Kyle Schwarber tore the ACL and LCL in his left knee after colliding with Dexter Fowler on a fly ball. After having surgery a few days later, he was presumed to be out for the season. (AP Images)

Defending Cy Young Award winner Jake Arrieta embraces catcher David Ross after throwing a no-hitter, the second of his career, against the Cincinnati Reds on April 21. It was the first no-hitter caught by Ross in his 15-year career. (AP Images)

Lefty Jon Lester had the best year of his career in 2016, going 19–5 with a 2.44 ERA. (Sue Skowronski)

Kyle Hendricks barely breaks 90, but used his intelligence to become a Cy Young Award candidate with a 16-8 record and an MLB-leading 2.13 ERA.

The wily veteran John Lackey provided a dependable arm for the Cubs 2016 rotation.

At only 22 years of age, second-year shortstop Addison Russell has impressed with both his glove and bat. He and his infield compatriots comprised the starters for the National League in the All-Star Game.

(Photos courtesy of Sue Skowronski)

At just 27 years of age, Anthony Rizzo has become the heart and soul of this young Cubbie ballclub. His 32 home runs and 109 RBIs for 2016 didn't hurt either.

Reigning ROY and MVP candidate Kris Bryant didn't suffer from a sophomore slump, leading the Cubs in home runs (39), hits (176), runs (121), total bases (334), and slugging (.554).

(Photos courtesy of Sue Skowronski)

After signing a lucrative free agent deal, Jason Heyward struggled at the plate. His defense, however, was top-notch all season.

"You go, we go": Dexter Fowler seemed to always be on base for the 2016 Cubs. (Photos courtesy of Sue Skowronski)

Second baseman Ben Zobrist, signed as a free agent, had a memorable game on May 6. Here he is crossing the plate after one of his two home runs of the day, to go with four RBIs. (Sue Skowronski)

Javier Baez is greeted by teammates after a walk-off home run to defeat the Washington Nationals on Mother's Day, 4–3. (AP Images)

s Bryant had a career day on June 27 against Cincinnati, going 5-for-5 with three home runs five RBIs.

r the young professional, teammates try to coerce Bryant into a curtain call at Great erican Ballpark after his stellar day at the plate. To his credit, and not wanting to show up home team, he refused. (Photos courtesy of AP Images)

Not known for his prowess at the plate, Jon Lester comes up with a pinch-hit walk-off sacrifice bunt to lead the Cubs in victory over the Seattle Mariners, 7-6, in 12 innings.

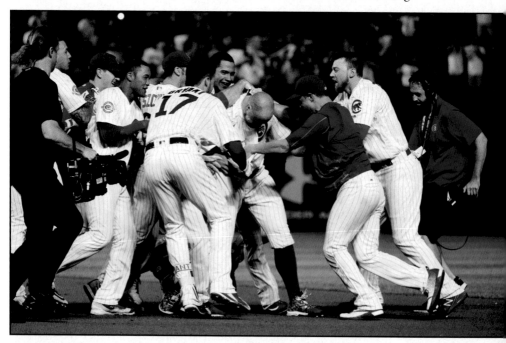

Lester mobbed by teammates after his game-winning sacrifice. (Photos courtesy of AP Images)

riving via trade from the Yankees July 25, the Cuban fireballer oldis Chapman took the role as oser for the Cubs and dominated, tting up a 1.01 ERA with 16 saves his limited time with the club.

A 15-year veteran, David Ross became the adopted "grandfather" of the young Cubs team. Deciding to retire at the end of the season, Ross was embraced by the Chicago faithful as one of their own—and the feeling was mutual.

All-around player Willson Contreras brought the kind of youthful enthusiasm every team looks for. As a mid-season call-up, Contreras played the outfield, first base, and catcher while putting up a .282 batting average. The sky's the limit for this young Venezuelan.

(Photos courtesy of Sue Skowroski)

For a team that's known more for losing than winning, records like this were set all season. With a young core and great management, these are no longer your father's (or grandfather's) Cubs.

The Cubs flag was flown at the top of the Wrigley scoreboard standings for all but one day during the 2016 season. (Photos courtesy of Sue Skowronski)

With a 103–58 record, winning the NL Central was just the first step on the road to greatness. (Sue Skowronski)

The Cubs take a team photo after eliminating the San Francisco Giants in Game 4 of the NLDS. (AP Images)

Miguel Montero smashes a grand slam in Game 1 of the NLCS against the Los Angeles Dodgers. The Cubs would go on to win the series in six games.

Cubs owner Tom Ricketts holds up the Warren C. Giles trophy after his team's NLCS victory over the Dodgers. Theo Epstein, the team's president for baseball operations and architect, smiles in approval.

(Photos courtesy of AP Images)

rigley Field before its first World Series game in 71 years.

thony Rizzo hits a two-run home run against Indians pitcher Mike Clevinger in the ninth
ing of Game 6. The Cubs would win, 9–3, leading to a deciding Game 7.

(Photos courtesy of AP Images)

After a short rain delay, Ben Zobrist celebrates his tiebreaking double in the 10th inning of Game 7, giving the Cubs a 7–6 lead.

Zobrist celebrates after being awarded the Series MVP trophy, helping the Cubs win their first World Series since 1908.

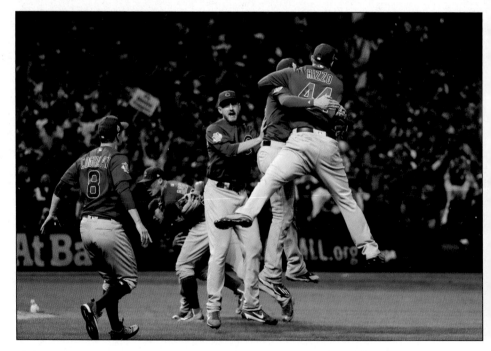

Cubs win!

(Photos courtesy of AP Images)

it back. That turned out to be a difference maker, as the Sox won 5–4 after blowing a 4–0 lead. Javier Baez's two-run homer in the seventh made it 4–2, and then Sox relievers gave up RBI singles to Dexter Fowler and Anthony Rizzo in the ninth.

But again it was failure from Montgomery, this time in a much higher-leverage situation than his Cubs debut, that cost the Cubs the game. He faced three batters, who produced a single and a sacrifice bunt before a game-winning hit by Tyler Saladino. Sox fans—who might have been a minority in the crowd in their own park—were happy, as it was the third straight game the Sox had blown a lead in the eighth inning or later and come back and won in walk-off fashion.

From ugly to bizarre—that described the second game at the Cell, before the series venue would swap to Wrigley. James Shields, who had a four-start stretch in late May and early June in which he posted a 24.80 ERA (not a misprint, that's twenty-four-point-eighty with 31 earned runs allowed in 11⅓ innings), threw 7⅔ shutout innings against the Cubs. He followed that start with another horrific four-start run, a 17.80 ERA, 27 earned runs, and nine home runs allowed in 14 innings.

And yet the Cubs couldn't touch him. Inexplicable. Shields became the third pitcher in 2016 to throw that many scoreless innings against the Cubs. The others: Madison Bumgarner and Gerrit Cole.

The series shifted to Wrigley, and things didn't start out any better. Career minor leaguer Anthony Ranaudo—who wound up with a season ERA of 8.46—no-hit the Cubs through 5⅓ innings, allowing just three walks. Not only that, he homered off Jason Hammel, becoming the first White Sox pitcher to ever homer off the Cubs since interleague play began.

This was not fun. What happened after that was, though.

Kris Bryant broke up the no-hitter, and the shutout, with his 26th home run. As Ranaudo's homer had been the Sox' only run, that tied the game. The Cubs continued the long-ball barrage with a two-run blast by Javier Baez in the seventh, and after Ranaudo was removed, ex-Cub Jacob Turner served up a grand slam to Addison Russell after an RBI double by Ben Zobrist in the eighth. Russell wound up having nine hits in 2016 with the bases loaded, the most of anyone in the major leagues.

Aroldis Chapman had been loosening up for his first Cubs save opportunity with the score 3–1 going into the bottom of the eighth. The five-run inning took away the save opp, but with Chapman having not thrown in four days, Joe Maddon decided to let him pitch anyway.

But Chapman hadn't thrown since Saturday, so Maddon likely figured he needed the work.

Chapman did something I don't think I've ever seen before when he first got up in the bullpen—he threw a dozen or so warm-up pitches with a weighted ball, not an actual baseball. This is apparently part of his routine for every game.

When he came into the game, the Wrigley crowd loudly and definitively showed they were on his side. He entered to an ovation and chants of "Let's go, Chapman!" and he proceeded to show why the Cubs gave up four players to get him.

He threw 15 pitches, 12 of them over 100 miles per hour, oohs and aahs heard from the Wrigley faithful every time that triple-digit number appeared on the video board. The 12 pitches over 100 equaled the total of 100-plus pitches thrown by all Cubs from 2008 through Chapman's arrival.

Chris Sale was to face the Cubs in the series finale. Always tough on the Cubs, they got through against him for a pair of runs in six innings, while John Lackey was holding the Sox to just one. One further unearned run off Nate Jones got the Cubs a 3–1 lead going into the eighth. With two out and a runner on second, Maddon summoned Chapman for a four-out save.

He got it, throwing 24 pitches, 16 strikes, and again thrilling the crowd every time "100" or another such figure appeared on the Wrigley video boards.

The win, giving the Cubs a split of the four games with the White Sox, gave the Cubs a 6–3 mark in interleague play as another

AL squad, the Seattle Mariners, came to town for the final three games of July. The Cubs needed to win all of them to avoid having a losing month.

The first game was a laugher. Jason Heyward (who surely needed it!) homered, as did David Ross, and the Cubs blew out Hisashi Iwakuma and the Mariners, 12–1. It got so bad for Seattle that infielder Luis Sardinas pitched the eighth inning. He was the only Seattle hurler to not allow a run, and he became the first opposition position player to pitch at Wrigley Field since Chris Donnels did it for the Dodgers in a 20–1 Cubs win, May 5, 2001.

That made another baby three-game winning streak for the Cubs and, including the win in the final game before the All-Star break, 10 wins in the previous 15 games.

But the Cubs couldn't keep it going the next day, and the loss clinched a losing month of July, the team's first losing calendar month since September 2014. The Mariners' Wade Miley didn't allow a Cubs hit until Kris Bryant singled with one out in the seventh following a walk to Dexter Fowler. A sacrifice brought Javier Baez to the plate with runners on second and third. Javy bounced to short; the throw came home and Fowler was called out, but the Cubs got the run and a 1–0 lead when the call was overturned on video review. Bryant went to third and broke for the plate when Miley attempted a pickoff at first. Bryant was called safe, but the Cubs lost this review, and the inning was over, instead of the Cubs having a 2–0 lead.

Jake Arrieta had given up just two hits over seven innings, but then he succumbed to something that had plagued him all season: walks. He walked the first two hitters he faced in the eighth. Hector Rondon entered and got a pair of outs, and again Chapman was called on with runners on base for a four-out save.

Leonys Martin timed one of Chapman's fastballs and slammed it into the gap in left-center for a two-run double, and eventually got wild-pitched in for the fourth run in a 4–1 loss.

After the game, Chapman let it be known to the media that he preferred coming in for only one inning at the start of the ninth.

You'd have thought this would have been discussed before he made a single appearance for the Cubs, though.

July ended with perhaps the most memorable game of the entire regular season.

It didn't start out that way. As part of Joe Maddon's desire to spread out his top starters' outings, the Cubs recalled Brian Matusz, another scrap-heap signing, from Triple-A Iowa to start this Sunday night ESPN-featured game.

To say Matusz was "awful" would be charitable. The Mariners scored two runs in each of the first three innings for a 6–0 lead. Each of the two-run frames came on a two-run homer, one each by Nelson Cruz, Robinson Cano, and Dae-ho Lee. And once again, a Mariners pitcher was working on a no-hitter, this time "King" Felix Hernandez, who, having actually thrown one before, might have had a shot.

I had pretty much chalked this one up in the "L" column and figured, "Hey, there's another game tomorrow."

With one out in the fifth and a runner on base, Dexter Fowler broke up the nascent no-no with a single. That seemed to unglue King Felix. He issued another walk, loading the bases, before striking out Anthony Rizzo for the second out. But then Ben Zobrist walked, forcing in a run, and Miguel Montero was hit by a pitch, scoring a second run.

Hmm, I thought. 6–2 after five? Well, it's interesting, at least.

After Joe Nathan gave up a walk and a double in the sixth (in his final appearance as a Cub, as it turned out), Travis Wood got out of that inning.

Then Joe Maddon's managerial gears went into overdrive. Pedro Strop entered to pitch the seventh, but instead of leaving the game, Wood went to left field, for the second time in 2016. Wouldn't you know it, with a runner on base, a ball hit by Franklin Gutierrez headed Wood's way, almost to the wall in left-center field. With his back nearly to the ivy, Wood reached up and made the catch. Bleacher fans began bowing down to him. Wood later told reporters: "Last time I went out there, I didn't get to make an out. I was hoping it would be less dramatic." Jason Heyward added: "Not many left fielders make that play because they would've been afraid," of the brick wall behind the ivy, presumably.

Ben Zobrist tripled in a run in the bottom of the inning to make it 6–3.

Strop began the eighth by allowing a leadoff double. With two out, Wood then reentered to pitch, with Matt Szczur replacing him in the outfield. He didn't even have to retire a batter, as he picked Shawn O'Malley off base to end the inning.

The Cubs had two singles in the bottom of the eighth, bringing the tying run to the plate in the form of Javier Baez. But Edwin Diaz struck out Baez and Dexter Fowler, sending the game to the ninth with the Cubs still down by three.

It was about that time I saw my friend Jeff walking on the concourse behind me, ready to head down the stairs to go home. I have a standing joke with friends I see departing games that seem to be lost in the late innings. As they walk behind my seat to the exit, I say, "But you'll miss the big comeback!"

We share a laugh, and the game moves on, most times to defeat.

Except Sunday night, it didn't. (And I got a postgame text from Jeff saying, "Well, you called it! I messed up tonight!")

I did call it, but I had done this literally hundreds of times without being right. A double by Anthony Rizzo and a single by Zobrist again brought the tying run to the plate. Addison Russell singled in Rizzo and Zobrist went to third, with Russell taking second on the throw in. Jason Heyward was hit by a pitch to load the bases, and Willson Contreras hit into a force play, which scored the second run of the inning.

It was nearly a game-ending double play. Contreras just beat the relay throw; Mariners manager Scott Servais challenged, but the call on the field was upheld.

It's now 6–5 with two out and runners on first and third.

And Mariners closer Steve Cishek, who has an exaggerated submarine pitching style, threw a wild pitch, scoring Russell, and the game was tied.

No one reached base in the 10th or 11th, scoreless frames from Aroldis Chapman and Hector Rondon. In the top of the 11th, Contreras made a sliding grab of a sinking liner in short left field. The Cubs used five different players in left field in this game, in this order: Chris Coghlan, Wood, Matt Szczur, Zobrist, and Contreras, and two of them—Wood and Contreras, neither an outfielder by trade—made outstanding defensive plays. In the top of the 12th, Russell saved a hit with a sliding pickup and quick throw on a hard grounder by Guillermo Heredia.

And on the game moved to the bottom of the 12th, the Wrigley scoreboard clock well past 11:00.

Heyward doubled to deep right-center, a ball that didn't miss being a walk-off homer by much. Contreras hit a fly ball that advanced Heyward to third.

Jon Lester then stepped to the plate. The Cubs were out of position players—and pitchers, too. John Lackey had begun to warm up to come into the game had it gone to the 13th.

Every single player on both benches, and everyone in the ballpark (about half the sellout crowd had stuck around for the end of this one), knew what Lester was up there to do: bunt, to try to squeeze the winning run home.

Jon Lester, who was bad at hitting and almost worse at bunting when he first came to the Cubs.

But Lester worked hard at becoming a better bunter; in one 2015 game, he had three sacrifice bunts, only the fifth time in all of Cubs history any pitcher had done that.

He ran the count to 2–2 and then laid down a perfect squeeze, scoring Heyward and creating a wild scene in which rosin bags and water were thrown, Cubs players and fans delirious at this crazy, fantastic, late-night win.

Consider:

- It was the Cubs' first walk-off bunt since May 11, 1988, when Vance Law did it against the Padres in the 10th inning for a 1–0 win.

- It was the first time the Cubs had come back to win after being six runs down since August 30, 2012, against the Brewers, when they trailed 9–3 going into the bottom of the sixth.
- It was the first time any Cubs team had won a game *trailing by three going into the bottom of the ninth* since September 18, 2008, also against the Brewers, a game they were behind by *four runs* (6–2) entering the last of the ninth. A Jim Edmonds single made it 6–3, and with two out, Geovany Soto hit a three-run, game-tying homer.
- According to ESPN, the Cubs had lost 371 games since then when they trailed by at least three going into the last of the ninth.
- And the score of that 2008 game? 7-6. In 12 innings. You can't make this stuff up.

And after all that, Brian Matusz, who started one game for the champion 2016 Cubs and didn't even make it to the fourth inning before being shipped back to the minors the next day, can tell his grandchildren the Cubs won the one 2016 game he started. Who writes these scripts, anyway? And it would only get wilder when August began.

Chapter 8

August: Winning, and Winning, and Winning

A pril had been the Cubs' best month of the season thus far, but they matched it—and more—in August.

The July 31 win over the Mariners wasn't part of August, but it was the beginning of the longest winning streak of the 2016 season.

August 1 brought another "M" team, the Marlins, to Wrigley Field for a three-game series. The first game of the set was the one that really set Kyle Hendricks on a Cy Young path. Hendricks had been decently good since the All-Star break, though he had been hit pretty hard the previous week by the White Sox.

On this night, though, he gave the Cubs exactly what they needed after the bullpen had thrown nine total innings the previous night after the Brian Matusz Blowup. Hendricks threw a 123-pitch complete-game shutout and became the first Cubs pitcher to throw a shutout and also have a hit, walk, and RBI at the plate since Kevin Tapani did it at Montreal April 10, 1998. And no Cubs pitcher had done that at Wrigley Field since Claude Passeau—76 years earlier on September 23, 1940.

More things that hadn't happened in decades. Hendricks barely breaks 90 on the pitch-speed meters but strikes out a fair number of hitters because he locates his changeup so well. The shutout put Kyle in the National League lead for ERA at home at 1.19. Also, Hendricks became the first Cubs pitcher not named Jake Arrieta to throw a complete-game shutout at Wrigley Field since Ryan Dempster did it against the Pirates September 29, 2009. As usual in games like this,

Hendricks had a lot of help from his defense; there were excellent plays made by Addison Russell, Javier Baez, Matt Szczur, and Willson Contreras.

The next night brought an event that turned out to be, sadly, historic, though we did not know it at the time. It was Jose Fernandez's first career start at Wrigley Field, and he'd shut the Cubs down in June in Miami. This time, though, they got to him for single runs in the first, third, and fifth innings and Jason Hammel allowed no runs in six—it was the bullpen that made this one close, with a pair of runs off Pedro Strop in the seventh. Aroldis Chapman again shut things down with triple-digit heat, and the Cubs had a 3–2 win.

No one knew that Fernandez would die in a horrifying boat accident only seven weeks later, and so his first Wrigley start wound up being his only one. I'm glad I got to see him pitch in person once.

The Cubs completed the sweep and ran their winning streak to four on a sunny Wednesday when John Lackey wasn't sharp. They went into the ninth trailing, 4–2, but Miguel Montero led off the ninth with a double off Marlins closer A.J. Ramos and Javier Baez singled him to third. Matt Szczur walked to load the bases, and Dexter Fowler's sacrifice fly made it 4–3 and, significantly, the other runners also advanced.

Throughout this inning, my friend Dave kept saying, "He's going to throw a wild pitch," referring to Ramos, who'd run three-ball counts to three straight hitters (after Montero's double, which was on the first pitch of the inning). It didn't happen when Kris Bryant batted, although Ramos ran the count full before striking KB out. Still, Don Mattingly left Ramos in the game, to issue an intentional walk to Anthony Rizzo.

Ramos's wildness continued with a walk on a 3–1 count to Ben Zobrist, which tied the game.

That's when Dave turned out to be prescient. Ramos threw strike one to Willson Contreras and, finally, bounced his 35th pitch of the inning in the dirt, far away from catcher Jeff Mathis, and Szczur scored the winning run, producing the Cubs' second wild walk-off win in four days.

Finally, for the first time in a month, the Cubs got on an airplane as a team and flew cross country to face the Oakland Athletics. Would the time zone change—even with an off day—affect them?

It certainly didn't affect Jorge Soler, who was activated from the disabled list to DH in this series. This activation also marked the end of Joe Nathan's Cubs career, as he was designated for assignment to make room for Soler. Dexter Fowler led off this game with a home run, and two singles were then interspersed with a pair of outs. Up came Soler, who hit the third pitch he saw into the Oakland Coliseum seats for a three-run homer.

That made things easy for Jon Lester, who had pitched two months for the A's in 2014 and wound up as the losing pitcher in that year's AL wild-card game before signing as a free agent with the Cubs. The reaction to Lester from the fans there was: meh, he was barely remembered, and besides, there might have been more Cubs fans than A's fans in the Oakland crowd. Lester gave up two runs in seven innings, and the Cubs had an easy 7–2 win, their fifth straight.

Saturday afternoon, August 6, was a throwback uniform day for the A's. They wore early 1980s garb, and the Cubs countered with their 1978–81 road uniforms. I never cared for these much when they were the official uniform; the white pinstripes on baby blue got them dubbed "pajamas" by fans back in the day, but as a retro throwback uni, they were actually kind of charming.

The A's were a better team than the Cubs for part of that era—they made the postseason in 1981, for example, while the Cubs were the worst team in baseball—but fortunes were reversed for this game, and series. The Cubs got eight strong shutout innings from Jake Arrieta (three hits allowed), and the 4–0 win was the Cubs' sixth in a row.

They made it seven and another series sweep as they wrapped up their quick three-day jaunt to Oakland on August 7. Hendricks, again, was solid, the only run off him a seventh-inning homer to Marcus Semien, and Soler went deep again for the Cubs, as did Kris Bryant.

Oddly enough, after the Cubs shipped off several of their better prospects in an attempt to improve their late-inning relief corps, it took until the eighth inning of the third game of the series against the A's before they used any of their key late-inning relief pitchers in that series, getting scoreless outings from Pedro Strop and Aroldis Chapman.

Another off day followed this series, to fly home from the West Coast. This has become somewhat of a staple of modern baseball scheduling, due to the vagaries of interleague play. The Cubs play the A's only once every three years, and thus when it comes time for either team to visit the other's park, the series often gets squished in between homestands. With two time zones and 2,000 miles in between, the schedule makers accommodate with off days on either side.

It's not pretty, but until and unless MLB makes adjustments in scheduling, this is the way it's going to be.

And so it was back to Wrigley again, to another one of MLB's wacky interleague-forced series, this one against the Angels. Interleague schedules consist of a four-game series (two at each park) against a designated "rival," three games each against four of the five teams in a designated division in the other league, and four games, two in each park, against the fifth team in that division.

The Angels got that "privilege" in 2016. But the two games in Anaheim opened the season for the Cubs, and the other two got squeezed into a homestand that would otherwise host Cubs divisional rivals.

Despite the presence of one of the best players on the planet, Mike Trout, the Angels weren't a very good team in 2016, largely because their starting pitching was awful. And the Cubs carved through it in this pair of games, routing them 5–1 in the opener behind homers by Willson Contreras and Kris Bryant off Jered Weaver, who used to be good but whose fastball in 2016 was even slower than Kyle Hendricks's (and he couldn't locate it as well). John Lackey had one of his best starts of the year, throwing eight innings and giving the Angels just three hits.

The Angels barely showed up for the second game of the series either. Jason Hammel threw seven shutout innings and Addison Russell homered in a 3–1 victory, the Cubs' ninth in a row. The Cubs swept the Angels in the four games they played and outscored them, 23–3. It was almost unfair. (Note, I said "almost." Anything the Cubs can do these days to dominate, I figure, is payback for all the decades of losing.) Unfortunately, the Cubs suffered a key loss even in winning this game. Pedro Strop slipped and fell trying to field a dribbler by Yunel Escobar in the seventh inning. He had to be helped off the field, and the MRI confirmed the worst. He'd suffered a torn meniscus and wouldn't return till near the end of the regular season.

The sweep of the Angels ran the Cubs' record in interleague games to 13–4, and they led the Cardinals by 12 games in the division, as those arch-rivals came to Wrigley for a four-game series.

The Cardinals—the Cubs' arch-rivals. It seemed as if the teams had switched places from 2015 at this point in the 2016 season— the Cubs blowing away the competition as the Cardinals had done the previous year in a 100-win season, the Cardinals trying to hang on for a wild-card spot.

If the Cubs could continue the winning streak and sweep the series, they'd lead by an almost insurmountable 16 games. On the other hand, the Cardinals were hoping to sweep the Cubs and cut the lead to eight—and even that would be a pretty big lead to overcome with 46 games remaining.

The Cubs won the first game of the series, 4–3, on a walk-off walk to Anthony Rizzo in the 11th inning, and they were probably lucky to get that, as the @CubsUmp Twitter account put Zach Duke's 3–2 pitch right in the middle of the strike zone.

You know, the Cubs had 108 years of breaks coming to them. We'll take it.

The game had lots of fun little quirks, such as Chris Coghlan trying to call time, not getting it, and slapping a single to right field in the sixth inning with the bases loaded. That drove in two runs and tied the game, 2–2, and David Ross followed with a perfect squeeze bunt to give the Cubs the lead. Randal Grichuk tied it up with a homer off Travis Wood, but the Cubs' pen held the Cardinals down until they could load the bases in the 11th for the walk-off walk.

The lead was 13 games. The next afternoon, the Cubs pounded former nemesis Adam Wainwright, chasing him after just two innings in which he allowed nine hits and seven runs. Good thing, too, because Jake Arrieta wasn't sharp. He allowed only one run in $5\frac{2}{3}$ innings but took 105 pitches to do so and ran lots of long counts.

Fortunately, the Cubs put this one away with two in the sixth and four in the seventh off former Cub Jerome Williams, who almost literally was throwing batting practice. The Cubs homered four times off Williams, two of those by Matt Szczur, who drove in three runs and scored four, the best day of his career. You might say he "szczed" the day, if you are into bad puns.

The lead was 14 games, the biggest of the season. Too early to start counting a magic number for division clinching? On August 12, maybe—but the number had been reduced to 34, pretty low for not even halfway through August.

Or maybe I shouldn't have mentioned that. The Cubs had bullpen failures in each of the next two games. Saturday, August 13, they took a 2–1 lead into the seventh on yet another fine start by Kyle Hendricks, who struck out 12, most of them on changeups that made Cardinals hitters look silly. A one-out homer by Jedd Gyorko tied the game 2–2, and at 100 pitches, it was time for Hendricks to leave for a pinch-hitter.

It was 2–2 in the eighth. The Cubs had many situations like that all year, and Carl Edwards Jr. was the perfect bullpen guy to relieve Hendricks, who peaks at 90. Carls Jr. (a perfect nickname!) can throw 95-plus. Unfortunately, on this day that 95-plus fastball couldn't find the zone. Walks and wild pitches put CJ in trouble, one run scoring on a wild one, and after more walks filled the bases, Joe Smith relieved Edwards. When I saw Smith warming up in the bullpen, I had even said to Mike, "This sight"—pointing to Smith—"does not fill me with confidence."

Turned out that feeling was correct. Smith had not been effective since coming to the Cubs, and this day was no exception. Randal Grichuk unloaded the bases with a grand slam. The Cubs managed a couple of consolation runs in the ninth, but the 8–4 loss ended the winning streak at 11. For Smith, that made five appearances, 3⅓ innings pitched, six hits, two walks (2.400 WHIP), and three home runs allowed.

Ugh. You could have chosen a random 20-something from the stands at Wrigley to take the mound, and he could hardly have done worse. The loss ended the winning streak at 11, which matched a 2015 streak for the team's second-longest since 1970.

And it got worse the next night, in front of an ESPN national TV audience. John Lackey again had a good outing but left the game with two out in the seventh after allowing just one unearned run. You could see him stretching out his shoulder and grimacing. When he left, the Cubs had a 3–1 lead, which Justin Grimm preserved with a strikeout.

The Cubs even had their bullpen set up properly, the way management envisioned it when they acquired Aroldis Chapman: Hector Rondon for the eighth, Chapman for the ninth. Hector was throwing for the first time in 12 days after reporting tricep soreness. He'd pronounced himself "100 percent" before the game.

"100 percent of what?" is a reasonable question to have asked after Rondon's poor outing. Kolten Wong hit a line-drive single, Hector couldn't field a bunt attempt, and then Stephen Piscotty hit a three-run homer. Joe probably should have replaced Hector with Travis Wood after that blow, which gave the Cardinals a 4–3 lead. But he left Hector in to face Matt Carpenter, who grounded out. Still no Travis to face the left-handed-hitting Brandon Moss.

Boom! Another homer made it 6–3, and only then did Joe replace Rondon with Wood. Finally, the inning ended. Anthony Rizzo led off the bottom of the eighth with a homer, making it 6–4, but that was all the scoring. Chapman came in to throw an uneventful 1-2-3 ninth.

"Uneventful" turned out to put the Cubs in damage-control mode the following morning on what should have been a dull, boring off day. It turned out that after Chapman's usual entry music ("Wake Up" by Rage Against the Machine), the Wrigley Field DJ who plays between-inning music played a song called "Smack My Bitch Up" by the British big beat band The Prodigy.

Well, if that wasn't the worst idea of the year, it was right up there. The horrified Cubs quickly fired the DJ, and President of Baseball Operations Crane Kenney issued this statement: "We apologize for the irresponsible music selection during our game last night. The selection of this track showed a lack of judgment and sensitivity to an important issue. We have terminated our relationship with the employee responsible for making the selection and will be implementing stronger controls to review and approve music before public broadcast during our games."

I can't imagine what this DJ was thinking. Kudos to the Cubs for acting swiftly and saying what needed to be said on this topic.

That news dominated the off day before the Milwaukee Brewers came to town for a split doubleheader, the day game a makeup of the April 27 rainout.

Trevor Cahill was activated under MLB's 26th-man rule (teams can add a player for a doubleheader without taking anyone off the roster) to start this game, though coming off a knee injury, he wasn't expected to go too far. Cahill surprised everyone by throwing five shutout innings, allowing just two hits. Mike Montgomery threw two scoreless frames, and Hector made up, sort of, for his poor Sunday outing with a scoreless inning. The 4–0 win was notable for the major-league debut of a Brewers pitcher who probably had had his fill of being teased about his name all his life, and far be it from me to not do that here. We had our share of laughs when Damien Magnifico entered the game.

Not just having the last name "Magnifico," seemingly more suited for a Borscht Belt magician, but the first name Damien. Much mirth followed.

Mr. Magnifico wasn't. He walked the first major-league hitter he saw, Ben Zobrist. The second batter of the inning, Addison Russell, was given a Magnifico Plunk. Damien the Magnifico then wild-pitched both runners up, where Zobs scored on a sacrifice fly.

Not as much fun was made during the night game about Brewers pitcher names—oh, all right, you talked me into it. Chase Anderson was chased—actually, literally, hit—out of the game by a line drive off the bat of Kris Bryant that hit him on his knee with two out in the first inning. The Cubs scored a run off his replacement, Jhan Marinez (whose biggest claim to fame, other than his oddly spelled first name, is that he was once traded from the Marlins to the White Sox for manager Ozzie Guillen), and later extended the lead to 4–0 off Milwaukee reliever Rob Scahill.

Jason Hammel threw seven outstanding innings, and the only real quibble I had with this one was Travis Wood serving up a two-out homer in the ninth, followed by a single. That brought Aroldis Chapman into the game, as it was now a save situation. Chapman wasn't real sharp; he issued a walk and threw a wild pitch but finished the game. The save made Chapman the first Cubs pitcher to save both games of a doubleheader since Jeff Fassero did it on April 18, 2001.

That's pretty cool, but if Wood had finished the shutout, it would have been the first Cubs doubleheader shutout in more than 50 years, since they blanked the Cardinals twice on July 11, 1965. As it was, the one run in the two DH games was the fewest in a Cubs twin bill since they gave the Mets one run in 3–0 and 5–1 wins at Shea Stadium on July 29, 1984.

Complaining about that, I know: #firstplaceproblems.

Anthony Rizzo, not long after the first anniversary of his famous "tarp catch," which the Cubs commemorated with a bobblehead, made a nearly identical grab of a foul ball in the seats by Keon Broxton. Then he jumped over the tarp back onto the field, as if he did this sort of thing all the time. Which, come to think of it, he sort of does.

More good pitching, and winning, followed the next day, 6–1 over the Brewers, featuring home runs by Jorge Soler and David Ross. Soler's first-inning, three-run blast would by itself have been enough to win the game. The Cubs had a fair number of these during the season, night games that were over almost before the sun went down. Ross's homer, at age 39 years, 151 days, made him the oldest Cubs catcher to homer in 56 years, since Jim Hegan hit one at age 39 years, 301 days on May 30, 1960.

It's numbers like this that connect the generations, if you'll indulge me a bit of a tangent off that fun fact. Jim Hegan was one of those guys the Cubs picked up late in his career in those days, hoping to grab just one bit more of performance. Hegan was the starting catcher for the Indians for a decade from the mid-1940s through the mid-1950s, the starter on their 1948 World Series-winning team and a five-time All-Star. Suffice it to say that by the time he got to the Cubs, he was about done. He played just 24 games in blue pinstripes, and the homer was the last of his career, hit in just his second game as a Cub.

I'm not quite old enough to remember that one, but I'm betting Cubs fans got briefly excited about Hegan, perhaps remembering his All-Star status. It didn't last long and neither did his Cubs career, as he was released two months later.

"Grandpa" Ross, just about the same age, and never as good as Hegan, provided much better performance. Modern Cubs management has identified players like Ross as being able to provide leadership and other factors to the team, while serving capably as a backup. Cubs management in 1960 was trying to recapture past glories.

The way they're doing things now is much better.

The Cubs completed the four-game sweep of the Brewers on August 18. They ran out to an early 5–0 lead, and Jake Arrieta had no-hitter stuff early, but as was the case for many of his late-season outings, he ran into trouble with walks. Two of them preceded a home run by Kirk Nieuwenhuis (really, it's time to figure out what got into this guy in 2016 when he played against the Cubs), and when Jake allowed a homer to Hernan Perez in the sixth and a couple of walks, he was replaced by Spencer Patton.

That didn't work; Patton issued a pair of walks, one forcing in a run to make it 7–5, uncomfortably close on a day that was sticky and oppressively humid. Bryant, though, hit his second homer of the day (and 30th of the year) into the center-field shrubbery and later drove in another run with a single, and the Cubs' 9–6 win was their 18th in their last 21.

And it could reasonably be argued that they could have won 21 in a row, matching their 1935 brethren, because all the losses in that span were from late-inning bullpen failures. Still, nothing wrong with an 8–2 homestand that left them 13 games in front of the Cardinals and with a division-clinching magic number of 30, heading to Colorado that they would celebrate on their flight to Denver with a pajama party, yet another one of Joe Maddon's "keep 'em loose" gimmicks.

It didn't work for the first Coors Field game, which had yet more bullpen failures, not seen by many in the Chicago TV-viewing audience, because the start of the game was delayed more than two hours by rain and then went into extra innings. It ended at 1:35 a.m. Central time. Yes, I stayed up and paid for it by being exhausted for the rest of the week, given that many of the other games on that trip were played in the Pacific time zone.

The rain, the Cubs couldn't control. The bullpen, supposedly shored up by the acquisitions of Mike Montgomery and Aroldis Chapman, should have been better than this. Travis Wood gave up an unearned run with the Cubs leading 5–1 in the seventh, and Carls Jr. had another rough outing, giving up RBIs to three consecutive hitters, tying the game.

Earlier, Kyle Hendricks had scored a run in unusual fashion. Hendricks, not usually a good hitter, singled and went to second on a Kris Bryant single. Anthony Rizzo singled and Hendricks headed home. Unfortunately, he failed to touch the plate as he passed by it. Plate umpire John Tumpane made no call, but the Rockies treated the play as if he had. Just to confirm that he had actually scored, Hendricks, looking like he was out for a stroll along the promenade, quietly walked back toward the plate (as he'd have had to go in that direction anyway to get to the Cubs dugout) and stepped on it to ensure the run. It would have counted anyway if the Rockies had abandoned the play and gone on to face the next hitter.

In the 11th, Dexter Fowler singled in a run and in came Chapman, whom Joe probably hadn't planned on using in this game. It was a rare bad outing. A one-out single by Nick Hundley was followed by a double from Ryan Raburn, and the Cubs had their first loss of the year in which they led by four or more runs.

What was up with Chapman? He didn't have his usual velocity: just one of his 10 pitches hit triple digits, and he threw mostly sliders to Raburn. Does altitude affect Chapman's fastball? He'd made one other appearance at Coors Field earlier in the year, while with the Yankees, and also didn't break 100 with three-quarters of his offerings that day.

Or maybe he just gassed after throwing in both games of the doubleheader the previous Tuesday and then having to throw 24 pitches Thursday in a game he probably shouldn't have had to be in at all.

The next night was better, as the Cubs reduced their magic number to 28—and yes, now that it was below 30, I figured it was okay to start counting—with a 9–2 win over the Rox. Mike Montgomery showed why the Royals spent a No. 1 draft pick on him; he no-hit the Rockies into the fifth inning. After the no-no was broken up by a homer from Nick Hundley, Trevor Cahill, who'd been retained after his "26th man" appearance during the doubleheader, finished up with 4⅔ sharp innings. Montgomery & Cahill (Law firm? Upscale grocery store chain?) allowed five hits, two runs, and struck out nine.

Kris Bryant, who was having a hot streak to remember, homered, as did Ben Zobrist. Bryant's homer was crushed—it went 469 feet and exited at 108 miles per hour. Even for a Coors Field homer, that baseball went a long, long way.

So did quite a few Rockies baseballs the next afternoon. Jason Hammel got pounded for seven runs in the first inning, though only three of them were earned due to two Cubs errors. With the bullpen being a bit overtaxed, Joe asked Jason to take one for the team. Hammel was finally yanked with one out in the fourth after allowing another homer. It was the second time he'd allowed 10 or more runs in a start in a little over six weeks' time. Rob Zastryzny (surely, the Cubs lead the majors in "players with at least one Z in their names"), who'd made his major-league debut in the first game of this series, looked pretty good in holding the Rockies down for 2⅔ scoreless innings with five strikeouts. Yes, I'm trying to avoid reminding you of the final score of this one. Suffice to say it was the Cubs' first series loss since before the All-Star break.

San Diego had not often been the site of Cubs successes. Even forgetting—and we'd all like to—the 1984 NLCS, the Cubs entered this series 19–24 against the Padres since the beginning of the 2010 season. They hadn't won the season series from San Diego since 2009 and lost two of three to the Pads at Wrigley earlier in the year.

Revenge on their minds? Maybe, as they swept the three-game set and outscored the Padres 16–7. In the opener, we saw our old friend Edwin Jackson, whom the Cubs were still paying in 2016 in the last year of the four-year deal he signed before 2013, the deal Theo Epstein said was a "mistake," a rare public admission of failure by a baseball executive.

Edwin did his old buddies and former teammates a solid in this one: three home runs, one by Kris Bryant, one by Addison Russell, and one by Jason Heyward. You might say E-Jax earned his Cubs money that night.

Jake Arrieta had one of his better outings the next night: eight shutout innings with just two hits allowed. The Cubs fashioned a

5–0 lead, thanks in part to more homers, Addison Russell joining Bryant this time. That gave KB four homers and 11 RBI in his previous five games, in which he'd gone 12-for-25 (.480).

The big lead led Joe to give the ninth to Felix Pena. Mistake! Pena gave up a walk and two hits, ruining the shutout. That meant Aroldis time, and he wasn't good either. A sacrifice fly made it 5–2, and after a walk, Chapman threw a wild pitch to make it 5–3. He finally ended it on a strikeout, which I barely saw because this was the third game of the trip that had ended after midnight Central time. My eyes were closed, and I was in dreamland right after that strike-three call.

Fortunately for me and my sleep needs, the final game of the series was played in the afternoon. The details of the 6–3 win were pretty ordinary: six more good innings from Kyle Hendricks, two RBIs from Ben Zobrist, and another homer (Willson Contreras).

But this game was significant for another reason: It moved the Cubs to 36 games over .500 at 81–45. No Cubs fan had seen a team that far over .500 since 1945, when they finished the year 42 games over at 98–56.

The Cubs' West Coast swing continued in Los Angeles, and it sure didn't help my sleeping habits, as the first game went into extra innings.

Joe Maddon gave Mike Montgomery another start, trying to get his main rotation starters more rest. He threw decently, three runs in five innings; but with four walks, he piled up the pitch count and had to be taken out after 91 pitches. Adrian Gonzalez homered off Justin Grimm to put the Dodgers ahead, 4–2, after seven.

That's when Kris Bryant took over. He homered in the eighth, and after a wild pitch scored Jason Heyward with the tying run in the ninth, Bryant gave the Cubs the win with a two-run homer in the 10th, to chants of "MVP! MVP!" clearly audible on the TV broadcast from a large contingent of Cubs fans in the Dodger Stadium crowd.

The run Bryant had begun with a homer in Oakland August 7 was what really got those "MVP!" yells going. From that date through this two-homer game at Dodger Stadium, Bryant hit .419/.470/.878 (25-for-74) with five doubles, a triple, nine home runs, 21 RBIs, and 25 runs scored. It was no coincidence that the Cubs went 14–4 in those 18 games.

In fact, this win closed out an incredible run for the Cubs. From the win over the White Sox at Wrigley on July 27 through this extra-inning victory over the Dodgers, the Cubs were on a 23–5 run, and it can be reasonably argued that only one of those five losses—the blowout in the final game at Colorado—couldn't have been prevented by better bullpen work.

Unfortunately, the Cubs didn't carry that winning through the final two games in Los Angeles. Saturday afternoon, August 27, they had another one of those games where Joe Maddon had seen enough Jason Hammel by the third inning. It's entertaining, to a point, to see the faces Hammel makes when Joe comes and gets him early. This time, it was after just 39 pitches and three runs allowed. Rob Zastryzny threw 3⅔ shutout innings to keep the game close, but they could get no closer than one run and lost 3–2.

The final game of the set was perhaps the most frustrating. Javier Baez thrilled us with great defense both throughout the regular season and in front of the national audience during the postseason. But on this day, he made a mental mistake that cost the Cubs the game. With two out and the bases loaded in the bottom of the eighth, Adrian Gonzalez hit a ground ball to Baez. Instead of throwing to first to get the slow-footed Gonzalez, Baez tried for the force at second, and Ben Zobrist, not expecting the throw, had to rush to get to second base, where Corey Seager beat Javy's relay. A run scored, the only one of the game, and the Cubs lost the series.

Was I thinking Cubs/Dodgers for a postseason matchup at that time? I'd be lying if I told you yes. The Giants, even though they'd gone 14–26 from the All-Star break to that date, were still only two games out of first place.

The Cardinals had cooperated over the weekend by matching Cubs losses with two of their own. The division lead remained at 14 games, the magic number now 20.

Western swings had been where past Cubs teams went to die. Whether it was the time-zone change, playing mostly night games where they'd been on a day-game schedule at home, or just not enough talent, many past Cubs clubs had horrific late-season trips out West that put them out of contention.

But the 5–3 trip here had the Cubs coming home for the final series of August with great confidence, and the possibility that they could, for all intents and purposes, swat the Pirates out of the division race.

The first game of the series started with a light rain falling. Most of the spring and summer of 2016 had been wetter than usual in Chicago, and the way things are in baseball these days, with millions of dollars tied up in every single game, they play through these instead of delaying or postponing them. It risks the health of the multimillion-dollar talent on the field, but with schedules as I've described them earlier, there really is no other way to do it.

The Cubs took an early 3–0 lead, then the Pirates started hitting Jake Arrieta hard, and they took a 4–3 lead in the sixth on a three-run homer by Gregory Polanco and extended it to 6–3 with two more off Jake in the seventh. But those are just dry facts. Here are the things that made this one wilder than usual:

- Arrieta battled through a 14-pitch at-bat and fouled off eight straight pitches before striking out.
- Arrieta later hit a long foul ball that came within maybe 15 feet of being a game-tying home run that would have been one of the longest home runs at Wrigley this year.
- The Cubs were three runs down going into the bottom of the eighth but tied the game on homers by Willson Contreras and Jorge Soler, the latter coming with one out in the ninth.
- The Cubs had not one, but two potential game-winning runs thrown out at the plate in extra innings.
- And, after 5⅔ excellent scoreless innings of relief by the Cubs' bullpen (granted, the two-run double off Travis Wood

scored runs that were not charged to him), the guy that gave up the lead in the 13th wound up with his first big-league win.

That was Rob Zastryzny, not even on the 40-man roster at the beginning of the season and not invited to spring training. But "All That Zaz" became an important component of the bullpen down the stretch.

Miguel Montero's 13th-inning single won it. Miggy had played so sparingly, and not well, over the previous month or so, so much so that he actually thought the Cubs might release him unconditionally. We should all be glad that didn't happen.

The next night, Kyle Hendricks stepped up once again, for the third time in two months, making a start the day after a game had gone into long extra innings and the bullpen was overtaxed. "All he does is get guys out," the mantra goes, and Kyle did it again, throwing seven shutout innings, allowing just three hits and a walk. Of the 23 batters he faced, just three hit the ball out of the infield. He impressed Pirates manager Clint Hurdle, who told reporters: "The command, the execution of pitches, I thought I was back in 1987 and it was Greg Maddux on the mound."

High praise, comparing Kyle (who began to pick up the nickname "Cyle" right around then, given the Cy Young buzz he was beginning to generate) to a Hall of Famer. Kyle's got a long way to go to match Maddux's career, but the approach is similar: pound the strike zone and locate your offspeed pitches. Watching Kyle strike out hitters with his changeup is a thing of beauty.

The Cubs completed the sweep of the Bucs, as well as the month of August, with a 6–5 win that shouldn't have been that close. The Cubs led 5–1 going into the seventh, and some sloppy bullpen work, including three wild pitches by Aroldis Chapman (a career first), made it a one-run affair.

Before that, Kris Bryant had launched his 36th home run of the season into the bleachers, and therein lies a tale. You probably couldn't see this on TV, but the ball bounced off a bleacher bench four rows in front of me, banging loudly and leaving a large dent.

After it bounced, it grazed the face of a friend of mine (who wound up wearing an ice pack for a couple of innings, thanks to quick work from the Wrigley EMTs) and landed directly in a blue plastic garbage dumpster that was, just then, being brought up the steps by two of the Wrigley clean-up crew.

The crew tossed it on the ground, where a nearby fan picked it up, one of the easiest home-run grabs you'll ever see in the bleachers. Incidentally, that ball was absolutely crushed, hit into a 17-mile-per-hour wind blowing in. If not for the wind, Bryant's home run likely winds up flying over our heads in the left-field corner and landing on Waveland Avenue.

The Cubs finished August 22–6, a .786 winning percentage that was their best in any calendar month (with at least 20 decisions) since July 1945 (26–6). It was the first time any Cubs team had won 22 games in a calendar month since September 1945 (22–10). The magic number dropped to 16.

And the best was yet to come.

Chapter 9

September: All the Ducks in a Row

"**A** September to remember" is a cliché, a tired old phrase, something I wouldn't ordinarily use in a book like this.

But that's exactly what September 2016 was for the Chicago Cubs. As wonderful and memorable as the rest of the season was, September's play topped it in many regards.

The first order of business was to take care of the San Francisco Giants, the team I thought would overtake the Dodgers and win the NL West. As in 2015, the Giants were visiting Wrigley Field for a late-season, four-game series. In that 2015 series, when the Giants were still within shouting distance of the Cubs for a wild-card spot, the Cubs swept and solidified their playoff chances.

The 2016 series was different, at least from a Cubs perspective. Far in front in the Central Division when the set began, the Cubs focused on knocking one number off the magic number each day. Meanwhile, the visitors from San Francisco were locked in a tight race for their playoff lives.

And what more appropriate way to begin than by facing old friend Jeff Samardzija, who was roundly booed when the starting lineups were given by PA announcer Andrew Belleson?

The Giants scored twice in the first inning, a two-run homer by Hunter Pence off Mike Montgomery.

And then the Cubs got to work on the Shark with one of their patented patient innings. Dexter Fowler, who just loves doing this, had a

13-pitch at-bat against Samardzija before walking. The rest of the inning consisted of wild pitches, hits, another walk, and you could see the steam coming out of Shark's ears. He threw 50 pitches in the first inning, and the Cubs had retaken the lead, 3–2.

Montgomery, as had been the case in previous outings, got himself in trouble with walks and lasted just four innings. That's when the bullpen stepped up. Rob Zastrzyny, Joe Smith (just returned from the DL on roster-expansion day), and Carl Edwards Jr. threw five perfect innings, striking out five, and the Cubs took the first game of the set, 5–4.

Magic number: 15.

Jon Lester gave that hard-worked bullpen the next day off, on an afternoon when the weather was absolutely spectacular, in the manner that early-September days often are: unlimited sunshine, gentle breezes, and temperatures in the low 70s. He took a no-hitter into the seventh inning, broken up when Pence homered. That was one of just three hits he allowed in a 102-pitch complete-game victory.

Thanks to the Reds defeating the Cardinals later that evening, the division-clinching magic number dropped to 13.

Madison Bumgarner, who'd defeated the Cubs in San Francisco, did it again at Wrigley the next day. It was a frustrating afternoon in which the Cubs got MadBum out of the game after six innings. They loaded the bases in the seventh but could not score, and it was made even more frustrating by a rare mental mistake by Anthony Rizzo, who walked leading off the inning. He was sacrificed to second, but when third base was briefly uncovered, he decided to take off and try to get there. Unfortunately, the Giants quickly got into position and threw Rizzo out trying to get back to second base. The Cubs lost, 3–2, the third straight game of the series decided by one run.

The final game of the set was the most fun we'd all had at a Cubs/Giants game in 2016, at least to that date!

This one gets a big tip o' the cap to Jason Heyward, who hasn't been mentioned much in these pages, primarily because well, he didn't do much that was positive all year. But on this Sunday afternoon, all the props went to J-Hey, who singled in Addison Russell with the tying run in the ninth inning and then, after both teams' exhausted bullpens wriggled out of trouble in the early extra innings, singled home Anthony Rizzo with the game-winner. The cry of pure joy from Heyward when the Cubs won the game seemed cathartic for him, as he'd driven in the team's first run of the day in the 3–2, 13-inning win.

The pitching staff as a whole was the real hero of this series. They allowed just 14 hits over the four games, a franchise record for a four-game series.

Heading on the road for a nine-game trip to Milwaukee, Houston, and St. Louis, the magic number was 11. The Cubs couldn't mathematically clinch until they got to St. Louis, and they'd have to get some help from other teams before they got there.

Labor Day in Milwaukee brought many Cubs fans to Miller Park, as any trip up I-94 usually does. Once again, Kyle Hendricks had his turn in the rotation on a day after the bullpen was over-taxed, leading me to dub him at the time the "Designated Bullpen Savior." And he did so again, throwing six innings while making only one real mistake, a sinker that didn't sink to Chris Carter, who homered. The game was close until the Cubs broke it open with a four-run seventh.

If you think Cubs fans don't get loud until the postseason, think again. Chants of "Let's Go Cubbies" were clearly audible through the TV broadcast, and Ryan Braun, a particular target of Cubs fans when he's at Wrigley Field, got booed. Loudly. Imagine how that must feel, being the subject of derision in your home ball-park. (Not that I feel a bit sorry for Braun.)

The Cardinals won again that day, so the magic number dropped only one number to 10. But they beat the Pirates, so they helped reduce the Bucs' elimination number to six. Imagine that, the Pirates, who won one more game than the Cubs did in both teams' great 2015 seasons and who were expected to compete for the division title in 2016, reduced to a third-place also ran.

I had made plans to go to Miller Park for the Tuesday game; the Brewers had a ticket deal, and I didn't want to deal with holiday traffic.

This was a mistake; the Labor Day traffic wouldn't have been as bad as the Tuesday game, in which Jason Hammel had a brutal first inning, allowing five runs after allowing the first seven hitters he faced to reach base, making me think: "I drove all the way up here for this?" Given the overtaxed bullpen, Joe left Hammel in to take one for the team, until, trailing 6–2 in the sixth, he served up a three-run homer to Braun—who got booed, again.

This would be the last regular-season away game I'd be able to attend in 2016, and almost incredibly, I had managed to somehow choose five road games to attend without ever seeing them win: May 19 and September 6 in Milwaukee; July 25 and 26 against the White Sox at the Cell; and the May 22 Bumgarner game in San Francisco. (I did better during the postseason fortunately.)

It wasn't any better the next night, although the score was closer. Anthony Rizzo homered, his 29th and third in two games, but that was almost the sum total of the Cubs offense. He also singled and so did Kris Bryant and that was it off ex-Cub Matt Garza and three Milwaukee relievers. Rizzo hit a ball in the ninth inning that was literally stolen from being a home run, as Milwaukee center fielder Keon Broxton leaped and reached over the wall in center field, bringing Rizzo's ball back from where it should have landed for a game-tying blast.

The schedule might have been catching up with the Cubs. They'd played two weeks straight since their last off day, and that had been on the West Coast. Thus, the September 8 off day in Houston was welcome, and so was Jon Lester's seven-inning scoreless start the next night in that former NL Central city. It felt odd to watch games in Houston, the scene of so many divisional battles until the 'Stros were moved to the American League in a 2013 realignment. This also meant the Cubs got to use the designated hitter for three more days, yet another chance to get at bats for Jorge Soler. He went just 1-for-4, and Kris Bryant's 37th homer of the season was the only offense the Cubs needed.

The win in Houston let the Cubs reach an historic landmark. It was the Cubs' 90th win of the year, giving them back-to-back 90-win seasons. That hadn't happened in the franchise's history since 1929 (98 wins) and 1930 (90). In fact, it was that 1930 season that perhaps set the tone for the entire franchise, and this leads me to an historical interlude that will explain, in part, some reasons for this long World Series drought.

William Wrigley, who'd acquired a minority share of the Cubs in 1916 and bought out his partners to become sole owner in 1921, had built a very good team, and they won their first pennant in 11 years in 1929 under manager Joe McCarthy. Wrigley thought they should have repeated in 1930 and fired McCarthy with four games remaining in the season, in part because of the 1929 World Series loss. Wrigley was quoted at the time as saying, "I have always wanted a world's championship, and I am not sure that Joe McCarthy is the man to give me that kind of team."

Well, Wrigley was doubly wrong. First, he replaced McCarthy with the irascible Rogers Hornsby, who was disliked so much that he, too, was fired—in the middle of the 1932 pennant-winning season. Meanwhile, McCarthy, quickly hired by the Yankees, went on to lead them to eight pennants and seven World Series championships in 16 seasons.

Things are better now under Joe Maddon. While the role of a manager has changed since McCarthy's time, Maddon seems to know just what buttons to push to get his players to perform at their best and to ignore all outside noise. Previous recent Cubs managers of playoff teams didn't get this. Lou Piniella seemed somewhat clueless with his 97-win team in 2008, and after the 2003 NLCS debacle, Dusty Baker was asked at the following winter's Cubs Convention what surprised him the most about that season.

His answer: "The goat."

That wasn't an answer from a man who understood how to lead this franchise to the promised land. Joe Maddon gets it.

The Cubs' offense nearly vanished completely in their second game in Houston. They got just two hits and one run off journeyman righty Collin McHugh, and a Cardinals win over the Brewers left the Cubs' magic number at seven. They'd have to win the next day (or have the Cardinals lose) to have any chance to clinch the division in St. Louis.

The Cubs did their part; Addison Russell homered and had three hits and Jorge Soler, again at DH, also homered. The 9–5 win made the Cubs 11–0 in games in which Soler had homered in 2016.

The magic number was five. A sweep of the Cardinals would give the Cubs the division title.

Kyle Hendricks was determined to not only win against the Cardinals, but to perhaps do something historic. He took a no-hitter into the ninth inning, the only St. Louis baserunners happening on walks in the second and eighth. Addison Russell and Jason Heyward made great catches to help preserve the no-no, and the large contingent of Cubs fans in Busch Stadium were loud, anticipating history.

Unfortunately, it didn't happen. Cardinals reserve outfielder Jeremy Hazelbaker, whose last name is two names in itself, homered leading off the ninth. That brought Joe out to remove Hendricks, but before he did, he'd asked Miguel Montero to go to the mound to talk to Hendricks, after Montero had already been out to talk to Kyle.

Plate umpire Joe West, who always enjoys making himself part of the show, told Maddon that would count as a mound visit. Joe didn't like that—rightfully so—and got himself tossed.

That wound up giving Aroldis Chapman the time Joe wanted him to get ready, and Chapman did enter to wrap up the 4–1 win.

Magic number: 3.

Unfortunately for Cubs fans who'd made the trek to St. Louis, the dream of clinching the division title there died the next day, September 13. The Cubs took an early 2–0 lead but then could not score again, leaving 10 runners on base and going 1-for-8 with runners in scoring position. They could have taken a bigger early lead on any of these opportunities:

- They had runners on first and second after Addison Russell's double with two out in the second, but Kris Bryant struck out.
- They had runners on second and third in the third inning with one out after two walks and a wild pitch. Russell flied out and Jason Heyward popped up in foul territory, ending that threat.
- They loaded the bases with two out in the fourth, all on walks, but Jorge Soler hit an easy fly to center field.

And they had just two other baserunners after that, so the best the Cubs could do after a 4–2 loss was clinch a division tie in the final game of the season in St. Louis.

Jon Lester—whose name is coming up more and more in these pages as a contributor when the Cubs needed him most—was the pitching and hitting hero in the matinee finale of the series.

Lester threw eight shutout innings and wound up driving in the only run the Cubs would need in a 7–0 victory with a little looping single into center field. That brought up this very odd statistical split:

Lester vs. Cardinals: 4-for-16, .250
Lester vs. all other teams: 4-for-98, .041

How does he do that?

The Cubs clinched a tie for the division title with their 93rd win of the season, their first NL Central championship since 2008.

They would head home from St. Louis and take on the Milwaukee Brewers in a night game while the Cardinals would be heading to San Francisco for a four-game series that would be important for wild-card hopes. The Giants had slipped in the NL Central race to five games behind but led the wild-card race by half a game over the Mets and one game over the Cardinals.

So either a Cubs win over the Brew Crew or a Cardinals loss to the Giants would win the division for the Cubs. The game at Wrigley was sold out, but you could still get in for $50 via StubHub—if you didn't mind standing room.

Fifty dollars to stand up for three hours of a baseball game. The price of winning, I suppose.

It's always nicer to clinch with a victory, but the Cubs "backed in," and I don't really like that term, but that's essentially what happened when the Cubs lost 5–4 to the Brewers, a few hours before the Giants eliminated the Cardinals from the NL Central race with a 6–2 win. The Cubs had a 17-game lead in the division and were the first team to wrap up a postseason spot. There was one magic number remaining—to clinch the best record in the league and thus home field throughout the NL playoffs (thanks for nothing, Bud and your "This Time It Counts" All-Star Game). That number stood at 10, over the Nationals.

So the atmosphere was festive and celebratory as fans gathered for the Friday afternoon game against the Brewers, but the Cubs struggled, going behind 2–0 early, tying the game on a home run by Albert Almora Jr. John Lackey was allowed to go just a bit too far and coughed up a couple of runs in the seventh, a two-out, two-run homer by Scooter Gennett.

With the bases loaded in the ninth, Addison Russell, to whom Joe had intended to give the day off, pinch-hit for pitcher Felix Pena. His two-run single tied the game.

In the 10th, Aroldis Chapman struck out the side on 11 pitches, and then Miguel Montero, who also wasn't supposed to play this day but entered when Jorge Soler departed with yet another minor injury, led off the bottom of the inning.

Miggy hit Blaine Boyer's third pitch into the left-field bleachers for a walk-off win that started a huge party, celebrating not just the win but the division title. The Cubs likely would have celebrated that title anyway after the game, but it was much, much more fun to do so after a win. If they'd lost, I'd likely have departed shortly after the game and not bothered staying for a weird, "Hey, we lost last night but clinched anyway, let's party!" celebration.

And remember my friend Jeff, who left early on the day of the huge comeback against the Mariners?

He caught Miggy's homer and came over to show it to me with a huge grin on his face, the ball a wonderful souvenir of this historic season.

The Cubs didn't do much better the next two days against the Brewers. The 11–3 score on Saturday, September 17, looks awful when you look only at the score and the starting pitcher, but the Cubs trailed just 4–3 when Jake Arrieta was removed after six innings and 102 pitches, and one of those Milwaukee runs was unearned due to an error by Tommy La Stella at third base. (Note to Joe: TLS isn't really a third baseman.) Relievers Carl Edwards Jr. and Spencer Patton got pounded for seven runs in two innings.

It didn't matter, right? The Cubs were still division champs. The score was closer (3–1) but the result the same in the final Cubs/Brewers meeting of 2016 the following day, most notable for being a rare loss in a Kyle Hendricks outing. From June 19 to season's end, the Cubs were 14–4 in Hendricks starts.

The Cincinnati Reds were next, and they were the Cubs' favorite punching bags all year. And in the series opener, the Cubs set a major-league record—though not of their own. The Cubs homered three times off Reds pitching, and the third, a two-run shot by Jason Heyward in the eighth inning, was the 242nd off Reds hurlers in 2016, the most allowed by any team in history. And as I noted to Mike after that factoid passed by on Twitter, the Cubs still had five more games left against this pitching staff. Willson Contreras's homer earlier in the game had hit off the 1030 W. Waveland building, right above the entrance, estimated by Ballhawk Dave as 463 feet, the second-longest by any Cub in 2016.

The magic number for clinching the league's best record and assuring the Cubs they'd play the wild-card game winner in the division series dropped to five.

And this is when I started buying up tickets for playoff road games. The Cubs could have three possible opponents in the first round, the Cardinals, Mets ,or Giants, as all three were still in contention for the two wild-card slots.

Cardinals tickets went on sale September 21. I had had an easy time of getting them in 2015 for division series games there, surprisingly so given the Cardinals' run of playoff years. It was just as easy to get tickets for the two possible games to be played in St. Louis in 2016, and that's only a bit more than a four-hour drive from Chicago.

Mets and Giants tickets would go on sale later in the week. That would require flights, and thank heavens for Southwest Airlines, which will let you cancel flights without a change fee. That meant I could book flights for both cities, cancel one of them, and still be able to use the money for another flight within 12 months.

There were more home runs to be hit against the Reds, though they didn't hit any in a 6–1 win in the second game of the set. That one was dominated by Jon Lester both on the mound (seven innings, one run) and at the plate. He hit a booming RBI double off Josh Smith, starting on a "bullpen day" for the Reds. The blast had an exit velocity of 107.1 miles per hour—where'd he get that kind of power? The wind was blowing in that night; otherwise, Lester would have had a real, regular-season homer to go along with his spring-training shot.

They did hit two more homers against the Reds in the series finale, a 9–2 win that completed the third sweep of the visitors from Cincinnati in 2016. Those homers tied a Cubs team record for the most home runs against a single team in a single year. The previous record, 37, was set against the 1955 Cardinals—in 22 games. The 2016 Cubs hit 37 against the Reds in just 16 games, with the final three games of the season to come in Cincinnati.

Kris Bryant's homer, his 38th, was a colossal moonshot. It would have been a souvenir for the Waveland ballhawks if not for a guy on the back concourse of the bleachers who made a terrific grab. What you didn't see if you saw the homer on TV was what I saw when I looked behind me in the bleachers—that man knocked over a trash can when he made the grab. Both fan and garbage receptacle survived the impact intact.

In the 16 games against the Reds to this date, they outscored them 125–55, the equivalent of winning every game over them by about an 8–3 score.

And then it was time to finish up the home regular-season schedule with three games against the Cardinals. When the schedule came out in late 2015, these games looked like they'd be important for the division race, but that was long over. Instead, the Cardinals needed the wins to stay alive in the wild-card chase.

Jake Arrieta finally looked like the Jake! we saw most of 2015 in the series opener. He threw seven shutout innings and struck out 10, and the Cubs posted another "not since" milestone by winning this game, 5–0.

It was the team's 98th win of the season, their most in 71 years. The Cubs had won 97 in 2015, and also in the 2008 division championship season, but not more than that since the last pennant year in 1945.

And when the Pirates later that evening defeated the Nationals, the Cubs clinched home field advantage throughout the NL playoffs. That was important, because I'd been chosen to participate in a presale of Mets division series tickets.

The sale was to begin at 9 a.m. By that time I expected to be in line at the bleacher gate for the unusual, Fox-TV-dictated 12 noon start.

Once again, my friend Ken, who lives across the street from Wrigley, came to the rescue. He wasn't going to be home at the time but told me that if I sat at a table outside his front window, I could use his Wi-Fi. Armed with the Wi-Fi password and my iPad, I sat there and within about 15 minutes ordered all the Mets division series tickets I needed.

Modern technology. Isn't it great? The previous day, thanks to Miriam winning the Giants postseason lottery, I had ordered tickets for those two games. So we were all set—we'd go wherever the Cubs went for their road games in the first round. And after another friend of mine told me Dodgers LCS tickets were still available, I picked up some of those, just in case.

The Cubs weren't so great that Saturday afternoon. Jason Hammel gave up four runs in the first inning and another in the second, and after he'd allowed two hits with just one out in the third, Joe had seen enough. If Hammel hadn't blown his spot on the postseason roster with previous poor outings, this one assured him of being nothing more than a cheerleader from the bench during October.

Hammel had been tentatively scheduled to start one of the season's final three games in Cincinnati, but not long after this bad outing vs. St. Louis it was announced that he had some elbow issues and wouldn't go. In reality, he didn't have a bad year for someone who essentially was the team's fifth starter: 30 starts, 3.83 ERA, 15 wins, 1.206 WHIP, 1.1 bWAR. Lots of teams would have had a guy like that as their third starter.

The regular-season finale the next night, televised as ESPN's Sunday night finale, turned into a David Ross party. Consider that Ross had been a backup catcher for most of his 15 big-league seasons, only once playing in over 100 games and having over 300 at bats in a season. But this year, with the "Grandpa Rossy" persona invented by Kris Bryant and Anthony Rizzo (and Rizzo had sent Ross a Father's Day card in June signed, "Your son, Anthony"), Ross became a huge fan favorite.

In yet another Hollywood-style moment, Ross homered in this one, a solo shot with one out in the fifth, to give the Cubs a 1–0 lead. With two out in the top of the seventh and no one on base, Joe Maddon came to the mound. Why relieve Jon Lester now? There's nobody out, the Cubs are ahead, 2–0 and Lester's thrown just 84 pitches.

Joe's trip to the mound, as it turned out, wasn't to take Lester out. It was to take Ross out, so he could get an ovation from the crowd, which is exactly what happened. That was engineered by Lester, who spoke to Maddon the previous night about doing just that. Lester did eventually come out a couple batters later, and after Carl Edwards Jr. allowed a run in the eighth, the Cubs got it back in the bottom of the inning for a 3–1 win.

That completed the best home season in Wrigley Field history. The Cubs won 57 games at Wrigley Field, breaking the previous franchise record (55) set in 2008. They fell just one win short of tying the all-time franchise record of 58 home wins, set in 1910.

All of this just felt like a huge awakening, as if the franchise itself had been sleeping since those long-ago years I keep mentioning here, like those were just a bad dream. The best part of this good dream was still to come, but it would have to wait nearly two weeks to begin, as the next home game wouldn't be until Game 1 of the division series against the wild-card winner.

Before that, the Cubs would have a final road trip to play two also-rans, the Pirates and Reds, and one more goal yet remained: get to 100 wins. The last home win had been the team's 99th.

They wasted no time posting win No. 100. It happened the next night in Pittsburgh in front of a crowd listed at 20,519, though fewer than half that many appeared to actually be in the ballpark. I almost (note: almost) felt sorry for Pirates pitchers, whom Cubs batters pounded for 18 hits and 12 runs, including Kris Bryant's 39th homer of the season. Kyle Hendricks threw six shutout innings, and it might have been a blanking except for a pair of solo homers allowed by Hector Rondon. That was a bit concerning; Hector was coming off an injury and hadn't really looked "himself" in a while.

The Cubs' 100th win—another "not since." This time, not since 1935, 81 years ago. You'd have to be into your 90s to remember that, and my dad told me he did, following all 21 games of that year's Cubs record winning streak on the radio, announced by Pat Flanagan. This was so long ago, it pre-dated WGN radio's long relationship with the team, which ended a couple of years ago.

The Cubs dropped the second game of this set, best not described in detail, as it was a poor outing from Jake Arrieta, and won the third. Before the game that day, news broke that the Cubs had signed Theo Epstein to a five-year, $50 million contract extension, with the entire management team retained, good news for the building of the strongest organization in baseball.

The fourth and final game in Pittsburgh became a footnote to baseball history.

It was played in poor weather conditions from the outset and, in fact, likely should have just been called off. The game meant nothing to either team, and the Cubs started Rob Zastryzny, making his first big-league start. The Cubs scored on a sacrifice fly by Tim Federowicz (this team has got to lead the majors in guys with "Z" in their names); the Pirates, on a sac fly by Josh Bell.

The game was stopped with one out in the sixth and an hour and 23 minutes later was called.

Since the game had no bearing on playoff positioning and it was the final game of the year between the two clubs, no makeup game was needed, and it went into the books as a tie. This is the only way a tie game can ever happen; in similar circumstances when there's another game between the two clubs, the game gets suspended and completed before the next contest between the teams.

So the champion Cubs have a tie game on their regular-season record, their first since 1993.

Then it was on to Cincinnati for more home-run fun to wrap the regular season.

In order to set up the rotation properly for the postseason, Joe and the brass gave a start to Jake Buchanan, who'd been acquired from the Astros in April and who'd toiled in Iowa's rotation all year, never on the radar for a call-up before September. He'd made one relief appearance early in September and then sat on the bench.

On the last day of the month, Buchanan put the Cubs on notice that they could consider him for a roster spot in 2017. Granted, it was "only" the Reds, but they still have some decent power hitters on that team and Buchanan shut them down: two hits in five shutout innings. Ben Zobrist homered twice, and that broke the Cubs team record for most homers against one single opponent, the 38th and 39th homers they'd hit against the Reds in 2016.

After a loss Saturday—and a poor outing from Jon Lester, whom you might have forgiven for having his mind elsewhere—the Cubs played their final regular-season game in front of a crowd that had to be two-thirds Cubs fans. Kyle Hendricks, trying to keep his ERA under 2.00 for the season, had a rough first inning (three runs) and departed after five, his season ERA still leading the league, but jumping from 1.99 to 2.13.

The Cubs went into the ninth inning trailing, 4–3, and the first two hitters were easy outs. Albert Almora Jr. drew a walk and Munenori Kawasaki singled. That brought Matt Szczur to the plate. Szczur doubled into the right-field corner, scoring both runners and giving the Cubs the lead.

Then it was Miguel Montero's turn. He hit a 1–2 pitch from Raisel Iglesias into the seats, and the Cubs had an improbable 7–4 win, their 103rd, the most for the franchise since 1910.

And to complete the improbable ending for the 2016 regular season, Montero hit the first and last of the Cubs' 199 regular-season homers. You predicted that, right? (No. No, you did not.)

It was the Cubs' eighth win of the year when they entered the ninth inning trailing.

And the best was yet to come.

Chapter 10

October: The Postseason to Remember

O ctober used to be a month where Cubs fans planned vacations to sunny beach resorts or to see historical sights in Europe, since the team nearly always went home for the winter after a poor regular season.

Now, October is a month where dedicated Cubs fans plan trips to other baseball cities to see their team in the postseason.

With the Cardinals eliminated on the last day of the regular season (huzzah!), I awaited the winner of the wild-card game to determine whether I'd go to San Francisco or New York for the Cubs' road division series games.

Miriam and I watched with much astonishment as Conor Gillaspie—nothing more than an average everyday regular, at best, in his time with the White Sox—smashed a three-run homer off Mets closer Jeurys Familia to put the Giants in the division series against the Cubs.

Thus it was that we cancelled our flight plans to New York (and used the Southwest travel funds to book a possible trip to Washington, thinking they'd take care of the Dodgers) and looked toward flying to San Francisco for Game 3 (and, possibly, 4) of the division series. Fortunately, my dad lives there—so traveling to a place that's normally quite expensive had no lodging costs.

One thing I felt very strongly about this postseason, after the Cubs got close but failed to make the World Series in 2015, was that they had to at least get there in 2016 or this historic regular season would have to be considered a failure. Harsh, perhaps, but when you're that good, and there's that much history to be overcome, I thought it was a necessity to take the next step and win the National League pennant.

Those thoughts came with me as I took the so-familiar trip to Wrigley Field for Game 1 of the division series against the Giants.

Despite having MLB-mandated reserved seats in the bleachers, we headed to the ballpark early. As usual, I wanted to be first in line, and beyond that, it's always fun to soak up the playoff atmosphere around Wrigley, as the quiet neighborhood comes alive pregame.

And the atmosphere inside couldn't have been better. Even though I knew some had sold off their division series tickets in hopes of making a profit to cover later rounds, those tickets had obviously been bought by rabid fans, as the volume level at Wrigley was definitely playoff-style.

Jon Lester put together one of his best postseason efforts. He allowed the Giants just five hits in eight innings, and though the Giants tried to take advantage of Lester's inability to hold baserunners, two of them were knocked off the basepaths by David Ross, who picked off one runner and threw out another trying to steal.

Meanwhile, Johnny Cueto was just as tough on Cubs hitters, and the game went scoreless into the bottom of the eighth.

That's when Javier Baez lofted a ball that I was sure was going to land on Waveland Avenue, or at the very least right on our bench—I could see it headed right toward me. But there was a strong northwest wind blowing in, and it knocked the ball down, lower and lower and lower . . . would it even make the seats?

It didn't. But thank heavens for the Wrigley Field bleacher basket, originally installed in 1970 to prevent fans from jumping on the field, which had begun to happen quite a bit over the previous year from the original yellow-helmeted Bleacher Bums.

Giants left fielder Angel Pagan, a former Cub, was stationed right at the wall, ready to catch the ball, when it landed in the basket right above his head.

Aroldis Chapman gave up a two-out double to Buster Posey but got Hunter Pence to ground to second base, and the Cubs had a 1–0 lead in the series. The game took just two hours, 30 minutes, the fastest Cubs postseason game since Game 2 of the 1984 NLCS.

The weather was still pleasant for Game 2, with temperatures still in the low 60s, but instead of a wind blowing in from left field, this time it blew in from right, a slight lake breeze. And it was old friend Jeff Samardzija starting for the Giants, again lustily booed when announced, as he had been just a month earlier during the Giants' regular-season visit.

The Cubs wasted no time in getting to Shark. Ben Zobrist hit an RBI single in the first inning, and the Cubs plated three runs in the second, two of them on a single by Kyle Hendricks—the first two-RBI single for a Cubs pitcher in the postseason since Mike Bielecki did it in the 1989 NLCS, also against the Giants.

Hendricks had a rough third inning, allowing a pair of runs to make it 4–2 Cubs, and his day got even worse in the next inning when he was literally hit out of the game. Angel Pagan hit a line drive that hit Kyle on his pitching arm. He seemed all right, even after taking a few warmup pitches, but was removed, most likely for the traditional "abundance of caution." This certainly wasn't the way Joe Maddon drew things up, having to replace a starter in the fourth inning, but fortunately, with Travis Wood in the bullpen, he had someone who could go multiple innings.

This, Wood did, and well, not allowing a run in an inning and a third of work, and he put the cherry on top of his outing by smashing a home run off Giants reliever George Kontos, a Chicago-area native. Both teams made multiple pitching changes after that, but no further runs scored, giving the Cubs a 5–2 win and a two-games-to-none lead in the series.

I was glad to have been at these games, as I prefer being at the ballpark to watching on TV, but I was especially glad after reading some of the reviews of FS1's coverage, particularly its choice of center-field camera location, which was from a platform built at the bottom-left corner of the center-field scoreboard. The Tribune's Steve Rosenbloom wrote:

> Fox Sports' broadcast of Cubs-Giants on its FS1 channel Friday night was a whole lot of odd, off-putting angles. The outfield shot seemed like the cameras were on the roof of Murphy's Bleachers and the replays came from Uncle Morris using his first iPhone.

Rosenbloom's comments were echoed by big-league pitcher Brandon McCarthy, who tweeted: "Is there a chance Fox doesn't have the rights to this game and they're actually pirating a security camera feed from across the street?"

Fox actually listened to these and other complaints and returned to the standard center-field shot, from the usual Wrigley camera shed, for the NLCS.

It was after those first two home games that I began to appreciate the travel schedule of ballplayers and beat writers, though the former always travel in first-class comfort.

It was not easy to turn around from a game that ended after 10 p.m. local time to make an 8:25 a.m. flight to San Francisco, even though Game 3 wasn't scheduled until the next day. And beyond that, Nationals NLCS tickets were going on sale at 9 a.m.—so I had to make sure that I could use the airplane Wi-Fi by that time so I could order tickets and be covered for that series, in case the Nats went on to win their division series against the Dodgers.

Fortunately, MLB's schedule makers had made the popular Cubs their prime-time attraction on both days, so the 6:40 and 5:40 local time starts would be much more convenient, not having to get up early on either day to head to the ballpark.

We were lucky enough to get a ride, from my dad's friend Patty, to AT&T Park for Game 3. That avoided the rush-hour crush on public transit and meant we wouldn't have to pay for parking.

AT&T Park is a jewel of a ballpark. You've no doubt seen the views of San Francisco Bay from there on TV, and they really did things right in building this stadium to have a feel of having always been there, even though it's just 16 years old. If a ballpark has the feel of the city it's in, I think the architects have done an excellent job. San Francisco has so many historic places and beautiful views and tourist attractions, and its ballpark fits into that West Coast culture quite well. Candlestick Park, the Giants' former home built on the edge of the Bay, was an atrocity—poor views, thousands of terrible upper-deck seats, and cold winds blowing off the water almost every night, though I won't ever forget Game 5 of the 1989 NLCS, played in sweltering 90-degree weather. The Giants did everything right in putting together their new park, and I salute them for that.

The Cubs, meanwhile, cared nothing for those sorts of things, preparing themselves instead for a possible sweep of the division series.

What they got instead was a defeat, but in a game that will long be remembered by fans of both teams.

The first memorable event was a three-run homer hit by Jake Arrieta off Madison Bumgarner—the first homer MadBum had ever allowed to a pitcher. The 3–0 lead, though, was short-lived. The Giants chipped away with a run in the second and another in the fifth, but Jake outpitched MadBum, allowing just those two runs in six innings.

And when Travis Wood and Hector Rondon got the Cubs in trouble by allowing a single and a walk leading off the eighth, it was Aroldis Chapman time.

This was somewhat controversial, given Chapman's stated desire to throw only one inning in games. Joe Maddon had stated that he'd spoken to Chapman before the postseason and the Cubs closer had assured the Cubs manager that he'd do anything he was asked in October.

The other issue was that Chapman is normally better coming in at the start of an inning. "Clean" innings are more desired by closers; if they give up runs, it's their own doing, rather than starting with someone else's runners on base.

Chapman struck out Hunter Pence, and that brought up the journeyman: Conor Gillaspie, still with the two runners on base.

Gillaspie hit a ball to nearly the exact spot where Jason Heyward had made a stunningly gorgeous catch in May. Unfortunately, Heyward had been double-switched out of this game, and Albert Almora Jr. was in right field. Almora is an outstanding fielder, but Heyward's better. Heyward might have caught up to Gillaspie's ball. Almora just missed it, and it went for a two-run triple, giving the Giants a 5–3 lead. Chapman walked the next hitter he faced and was removed, the first time he'd been lifted midinning as a Cub.

The Giants were three outs from their first win of the series.

But the Giants had put themselves in the wild-card spot, instead of winning the NL West, in part due to poor bullpen work, and they got some here. Sergio Romo walked Dexter Fowler, and Kris Bryant lofted a ball to left that looked like it was, as was Baez's the previous Friday, going to be grabbed by Giants left fielder Angel Pagan.

There is a gas-station ad on the left-field wall at AT&T Park. It shows three cartoony smiling cars. The one on the left juts out a bit from the wall and over the top and is a couple of feet wide. You know, the better to stand out.

Bryant's ball hit the top of that "car" and bounced into the seats for a game-tying homer. Pagan has to be wondering what he has to do to catch a fly ball hit by a Cub in this series. In the bottom of the ninth, Mike Montgomery walked Brandon Belt with one out, but a double play set the stage for four crazy extra innings.

The Cubs had no baserunners in the 10th, 11th, or 12th. The Giants had one man on base in both the 11th and 12th but could not score. Montgomery was actually magnificent, throwing four shutout innings from the ninth through the 12th.

In the 13th, the Cubs got two singles with one out, but David Ross hit into an inning-ending double play, and then Montgomery ran out of gas. He'd thrown 50 pitches from the ninth through the 12th and was now facing hitters for the second time. Brandon Crawford led off the 13th with a double and Joe Panik followed with another two-bagger, and the Giants had a wild 6–5 win, the game running five hours, four minutes, the longest postseason game in Cubs history both by time and innings. By the time it ended, it was 11:43 p.m. in San Francisco, closing in on 2 a.m. in Chicago, and the Cubs would have to wait till the next day to try to move on to the NLCS.

And that next day proved to be even more thrilling, more exciting, possibly one of the best games in Cubs history. It certainly was historic by anyone's postseason standards.

It didn't start out that way. John Lackey spotted the Giants a 1–0 lead in the first inning, and even though David Ross homered to tie the game in the second, Lackey did not seem as if he were going to have a good night, and he didn't, lifted for a pinch-hitter in the top of the fifth trailing, 3–2, after Ross's sacrifice fly previously that inning had scored the Cubs' second run.

Still . . . if the Cubs could keep this game close, maybe they could close out the series.

Justin Grimm and Travis Wood did not help matters by having rough outings in the fifth. Two more Giants runs scored, and, with the Cubs trailing by three runs, it appeared that they and the Giants were headed back to Chicago for Game 5. Matt Moore was dominant. Through eight innings he'd given up just two hits: Ross's homer and a leadoff single to Anthony Rizzo in the fourth. Rizzo was erased on a double play.

That's when Bruce Bochy made the decision that cost him the game and the series, though it was an absolutely defensible decision. Moore was removed after eight innings and 123 pitches. Only 23 times in the 2016 regular season had 120 or more pitches been thrown by anyone. Oddly enough, the pitcher leading that list was . . . Matt Moore, who threw 133 pitches August 23 against the Dodgers, because Bochy was leaving him in to work on a no-hitter, which he lost with two out in the ninth.

Maybe that was the reason Bochy took Moore out in this situation. Maybe he thought, "I overworked him then, I won't do it now."

They play "I Fought the Law (and the Law Won)" at AT&T Park when Derek Law enters games. He had not made many friends among Cubs fans watching Game 3 with his histrionics after every strikeout. In Game 4, the Cubs fought Derek Law and won—Kris Bryant singled. Enough Law, said Bochy—in came Javier Lopez because those pesky unwritten rules of baseball say you never ever ever use a righty against a left-handed hitter in situations like this. Lopez walked Anthony Rizzo.

Out came Bochy for another change, even though a switch-hitter, Ben Zobrist, was due next. It was Sergio Romo to face Zobs.

Zobs doubled down the right-field line. Bryant scored, and the tying run was in scoring position. The look of thrill on Zobrist's face was something we'd almost never seen from a Cub—the look of winning.

Here came Bochy again, seemingly being paid for every foot he walked between dugout and mound. (Don't give the Giants any ideas, they'll sponsor it.)

Chris Coghlan had been announced to bat for Addison Russell. Bochy countered with lefty Will Smith, but Joe Maddon had never intended for that to be the matchup. Joe knew Bochy would likely make this move and countered with Willson Contreras, the matchup he really wanted.

How great is that—to see a Cubs manager outmanage a three-time World Series champion?

Contreras smashed a line drive past Smith into center field, and the game was tied.

Jason Heyward, another pinch-hitter, squared to bunt against Smith. There's still nobody out, remember.

Heyward bunted too hard. Smith threw to Brandon Crawford covering second for a force. Crawford is one of the best-fielding shortstops in baseball.

Yet somehow, Crawford's relay to first eluded Brandon Belt, getting far enough away for Heyward to take second. So the Cubs got what they wanted—a runner in scoring position, while giving up an out.

Here came Bochy yet again, for the fifth pitcher of the inning, Hunter Strickland. He got Javier Baez down 0–2, and then Baez bounced a ball up the middle, and every Cubs fan was yelling, "Get through! Get through!" (Well, I was yelling that, anyway. I know others must have been thinking it, if they weren't saying it.)

It did. Heyward scored, and the Cubs had an improbable, no, impossible, 6–5 lead.

Aroldis Chapman's three Ks in the bottom of the ninth, the last getting Brandon Belt on a 101- mile-per-hour fastball, were almost an anticlimax. The 5,000 or so blue-clad Cubs fans at AT&T Park jumped, yelled, and screamed as the Cubs won the series, with one of the greatest ninth-inning comebacks in postseason history.

It can be argued that this inning was the single most important one in modern Cubs franchise history. It showed both players and fans that miracles can happen for the Cubs, not always against them. It showed the resilience that the 2016 Cubs had shown all season long. And it gave them a postseason series win for the second straight year.

Much credit to the AT&T Park employees, who were friendly and efficient, and to Giants fans, who couldn't have been more gracious in congratulating us on the series win. I suppose that having three World Series titles under your belt can make you a bit magnanimous, plus the thought that the Cubs might be able to beat the Dodgers, a team Giants fans absolutely loathe.

One thing I like to collect is tickets, especially from big events like this. Many teams are getting away from hard tickets, a trend I don't particularly care for. The tickets I'd bought for the NLDS games in San Francisco were boring, ugly Tickets.com versions. I went to Ticket Services at AT&T Park and asked if they could be reprinted, having done this on previous occasions.

I was told that they'd do it after the last Giants postseason game and I could mail in the tickets. But with a few hours before the flight Wednesday morning, October 12 (good thing I changed the return flight from 6:25 a.m. to 2 p.m. I'd never have made the earlier one after the very, very long games 3 and 4), I thought I'd call them and see if I could stop by in person. They said yes, and so I went to the stadium, finding it eerily quiet, though I had to go through a magnetometer to enter. They reprinted the tickets on nice Giants postseason ticket stock, so now I have a souvenir that actually says "Chicago Cubs vs. San Francisco Giants" and the date and time of the game on it. (And they let me keep the other set, too.)

I did make sure to not wear any Cubs clothing when I did this. Happy that the Cubs won, but I didn't want to rub their noses in it.

Following that and a happy flight home, I would now have two days off before having to return to Wrigley Field for Game 1 of the NLCS. One of those days off back in Chicago was spent watching Game 5 of the Dodgers/Nationals series, as I was still hoping for the Nats to win. I had everything arranged for travel to D.C.—tickets, airfare, lodging with friends.

All that was missing was the cooperation of the Nats, who lost, 4–3. I won't completely blame the umpires, but Julio Urias of the Dodgers at one point picked Bryce Harper off first base on what was obviously a balk, so much so that Joe Maddon spent a fair amount of a press conference during the NLCS discussing this and making it known that "the umpires are aware."

I had purchased Dodgers NLCS tickets on a whim, never thinking I'd have to use them; now it was a scramble to get airfare to Los Angeles. Fortunately, there were Los Angeles-area friends willing to accommodate Miriam and me for the three days the Cubs would play there. The airfare, though . . . I don't even want to tell you what it cost on short notice. Suffice it to say, given the result of the series, it was worth it.

Before that was the return to Wrigley for Game 1 of the NLCS. The weather was pleasant, if a bit cooler than the previous weekend's division series games. Again, Jon Lester was on the mound for Game 1, and once again, he was stellar, throwing six innings and allowing just a wind-blown pinch-homer by Andre Ethier.

Meanwhile, the Cubs jumped on Kenta Maeda early. They had a 1–0 lead within the game's first eight pitches on a single by Dexter Fowler and double by Kris Bryant. Two more runs scored in the third. The first came home after a triple by Jason Heyward and a double by Javier Baez.

Baez was wild-pitched to third one out later, while Lester was batting. This put the Cubs in an obvious squeeze situation, and Lester is a good bunter. He squared, Baez took off for the plate, and Lester missed the ball. Javy headed back toward third, Yasmani Grandal fired the ball down there, and Baez turned back toward the plate.

It looked like a rundown was coming, but Turner's throw home was offline, and Baez had a steal of home, the first in the postseason since Elvis Andrus of the Rangers did it in 2010.

And it had been quickly noted that the last Cub to do it was Jimmy Slagle in the 1907 World Series—but no Slagle steal was noted in any of the box scores or play-by-play accounts of the game. Mike looked this up for me:

> The play in question happened October 11, 1907, in the seventh inning of the fourth game at Detroit. The game situation was: Frank Chance at first, Slagle at third, two out. Chance broke for second, deliberately catching himself in a rundown, Slagle broke for home and scored, Chance was the third out, tagged between bases as part of the rundown. The Sporting News Record Book, Neft & Cohen, and the Elias Book of Baseball Records all call this a steal of home.

Under modern scoring rules, this is not a stolen base; it's assumed to be a base advance on a fielder's choice, since the run scored while an out was recorded. In this case, it was the third out of the inning, but the run scored before the out was made. Contemporary newspaper accounts called it a stolen base; the rules regarding this were changed sometime in the 1920s.

So let's give it to Slagle, while noting Javy's daring baserunning, of which Joe Buck said on the FS1 broadcast: "The baseball IQ for this young man is pretty high." That, of course, is nothing Cubs fans didn't know previously, as Javy'd been doing this sort of thing all year.

The Cubs nursed the two-run lead into the eighth when, just as in Game 3 of the division series, the opposition threatened. This time they loaded the bases off Mike Montgomery and Pedro Strop.

Again Joe called on Aroldis Chapman for a "nonclean" inning, this time a much more dangerous situation, bases loaded, nobody out. Chapman struck out Corey Seager and Yasiel Puig, but Adrian Gonzalez then singled up the middle, just out of the reach of Chapman, to tie the game.

Wrigley Field, noisy and boisterous throughout the postseason, grew quiet. It wouldn't take long for that noise to return.

Ben Zobrist—so often the catalyst in the postseason—led off the bottom of the eighth with a double. After a groundout, Jason Heyward was intentionally walked. A short fly ball produced the second out, and then the Dodgers did something mystifying.

Chris Coghlan was sent up to bat for David Ross, and the Dodgers intentionally walked him—with first base occupied. Miguel Montero was on deck to bat for Chapman. What Dodgers manager Dave Roberts either didn't know, or didn't think of, was Miggy's regular-season splits: .221/.340/.387 (.727 OPS) against right-handers, .189/.250/.189 (.439 OPS) against left-handers. Roberts had lefty Grant Dayton ready to go in the bullpen.

But right-hander Joe Blanton stayed in the game. Roberts also ignored Montero's lifetime record with the bases loaded: 33-for-98 (.337) with three grand slams.

Boom! Make that four (though it won't be listed with those regular-season stats). Blanton got Montero down 0–2 and then left a slider in the middle of the zone. Miggy's grand slam gave the Cubs a 7–3 lead, and Roberts later said that he left Blanton in because Blanton had struck Montero out in Los Angeles in August.

We can always be thankful that Roberts made this key decision based on one at bat, perhaps the smallest sample size ever.

The huge, roaring Wrigley crowd was still standing and cheering Montero's homer when Dexter Fowler hit Blanton's next pitch into the bleachers for an 8–3 lead. Finally, Roberts brought Dayton in the game, and he retired Anthony Rizzo to end the inning.

The Dodgers scored a harmless run in the ninth, but the Cubs had a 1–0 lead in the series.

The next night was the night Cubs fans feared: Clayton Kershaw, likely the best pitcher in baseball, going against Kyle Hendricks, who had been pronounced "good to go" after a bullpen session in San Francisco, following the ball that hit him in Game 2 of the division series.

What we got was a pitchers' duel, on a night when the wind shifted from blowing out (it had helped Ethier's homer in Game 1) to blowing in off Lake Michigan.

Hendricks threw well. The only mistake he made was a homer served up to Adrian Gonzalez in the second inning. But Kershaw was better, seven shutout innings and a narrow escape on a couple of pitches: a loud foul ball hit by Anthony Rizzo with two out in the fourth, and a deep fly to center by Javier Baez in the seventh that turned out to be Kershaw's last pitch of the game. Had the wind been blowing the same way it had for Game 1, that ball would have landed in the shrubbery beyond the center-field wall. Instead, it was an out, and Kenley Jansen retired all six Cubs hitters he faced for a two-inning save.

The series was tied 1–1. Beating Kershaw wasn't going to be easy regardless; at least the Cubs had kept the game close.

Thankfully, when I booked the last-minute plane ride to Los Angeles, the only flight I could get on was Tuesday morning. This was scheduled to arrive just hours before the game, but it at least gave us a day off to rest before once again heading for jet-lag territory in the Pacific time zone. Since the place we were staying at was located in Covina, about 25 miles east of Dodger Stadium, we had arranged with another friend, closer to the stadium, to drop off our stuff (including my computer, which I didn't want sitting in the car in 90-degree heat!) before heading to Game 3.

The Dodger Stadium experience is so completely different from being at Wrigley Field, they might as well be on different planets. Wrigley's in a congested urban neighborhood, surrounded by apartment buildings, some nearly a century old, served by bus and rail lines, and many people bicycle and walk to the park—the latter category include some of the Cubs players and management who live in the neighborhood.

Try doing that in car-centric LA Dodger Stadium is a huge edifice with the largest seating capacity in the major leagues, 56,000. It was built in 1962, a time when "if some is good, more must be better!" was a common thought not only for sports, but for everything. Stadiums built in that era often had that many, or more, seats—but baseball people soon found that only gave you 10,000 or 15,000 bad seats you couldn't sell. The current thought is that the optimum capacity at a baseball park is between 40,000 and 45,000—just in Wrigley Field's wheelhouse.

Dodger Stadium is really only accessible by car, surrounded by acres and acres and acres and acres and I'm using that word so many times because the parking lots seem to go on forever. They try to alleviate traffic by assigning you to lots that are the closest you can get to your seat. It helps to some extent, but if you arrive late you're going to get stuck, which is why you often see Dodger games start with empty seats. And people often leave early; the TV shots of brake lights beyond the left-field wall has become a cliché. They've also set up areas for Uber pickups and drop-offs, a useful thing in 2016.

Fortunately, I arrived early enough to not have to deal with traffic coming in. The lots and the stadium both open three hours before game time, and that was enough time for me to take a look around a place I hadn't set foot in since 1988. Though the Dodgers have added high-end seating areas and clubs, the basic look of the place hasn't changed much, and they've added quite a bit of retropainted signage that pays homage to the Mad Men era the stadium was constructed in. I saw one bar that had an aluminum 1960s-style outside wall out of which I swear I'd see a Don Draper-type in suit and skinny tie walk any minute.

Game 3 wasn't any better than Game 2, despite the presence of perhaps 10,000 Cubs fans, some of whom (like Miriam and me) came from Chicago, others expats who live in southern California, including quite a few in the entertainment industry whose faces you likely saw way too many times on the FS1 broadcast.

The Cubs couldn't do a thing against Rich Hill and three Dodgers relievers. It was almost bizarre to see Hill, originally drafted by the Cubs and who had a good year for them in the 2007 NL Central title season but who had gone under the knife multiple times and had been pitching in indy ball just a year earlier, shut down a high-powered offense and look like a Cy Young winner. Jake Arrieta wasn't sharp, but it didn't matter, as Hill was dominant.

The Dodgers had a two-games-to-one lead. Would this one end the same way previous championship series had, in defeat and sadness?

While we were waiting for Game 5 to begin, the Dodgers played Game 5 of the American League Championship Series on the stadium video boards. When the Cleveland Indians defeated the Toronto Blue Jays that afternoon in Canada, they won the AL pennant for the first time in 19 years. If the Cubs could get to the World Series, someone would be ending a title drought of at least 68 years.

John Lackey and Julio Urias matched zeroes for three innings on another hot afternoon in Game 4, at which time it felt like the Cubs would never score again, when three singles produced a 1–0 lead for the Cubs in the fourth inning, and a groundout by Jason Heyward made it 2–0.

Addison Russell then muscled a ball over the right-center field wall, and it was almost as if the entire team and fanbase relaxed. Suddenly 4–0, it looked like this would be an easy win. Anthony

Rizzo made it 5–0 with a homer in the top of the fifth. Both hitters had been in postseason slumps—this had to be a good sign!

Lackey, though, made it tougher. He walked the first two men he faced in the fifth, and when Joe Maddon came to get him, lip-readers read a profanity coming out of his mouth, when he clearly said, "You have got to be fucking kidding me!" He looked like he was about to rip Maddon's head right off when Joe asked for the baseball.

Mike Montgomery gave up a couple of hits that made it 5–2, but the Cubs blasted Dodgers reliever Ross Stripling for five runs in the sixth and won, 10–2, a welcome blowout.

Two Cubs fans from Missouri, Jim and Amy, wound up spending the entire game standing behind us. We invited them back there the next day, and when the seats next to us emptied out during Game 5, we told them to sit down. They declined, saying they didn't want to mess with the mojo.

Before Game 5, Miriam & I met two old LA-area friends, Mike and John, at Philippe's near Dodger Stadium for lunch. John told me I had to go there because, as he said, "It opened in 1908. That has to be a sign!" There were dozens of other Cubs fans there, too, perhaps thinking the same thing.

No one messed with Jon Lester's mojo during Game 5, even though Dave Roberts had told reporters before the game: "We're going to get huge leads and try to bunt on them and try to get in his psyche a little bit." Instead of getting to Lester, this turned out to be unintentionally funny. For example, when Kiké Hernandez led off the first inning with a single and then jumped around on the base paths like he was trying out for Dancing With The Stars. If Lester could have turned off his game face and laughed right then, he probably would have. Lester's bigger beef was with the ball-and-strike calls of plate umpire Alfonso Marquez, who squeezed the Cubs left-hander several times in the early innings.

Anthony Rizzo had given the Cubs a 1–0 lead with an RBI double in the first. That lead held till the fourth, when Howie Kendrick doubled and stole third with one out. Adrian Gonzalez hit a weak grounder to Rizzo, who fumbled it briefly and took the out at first, Kendrick scoring. That bobble was actually advantageous to the Cubs. The ball was hit so slowly that Kendrick probably would have scored even with a throw, and then the Cubs wouldn't have had an out. With two out and nobody on base, Lester got out of the inning with a fly ball, and two innings later, Javier Baez singled and scored on a majestic homer by Addison Russell, giving the Cubs a 3–1 lead.

The Cubs broke it open with a five-run eighth, with RBI hits from Dexter Fowler, Kris Bryant, and a bases-clearing double by Baez—all the runs unearned because Dodgers pitcher Pedro Baez dropped a throw from Gonzalez allowing Russell to reach base to lead off the inning.

After that, Aroldis Chapman, who'd been warming up in case a save opportunity arose, came in anyway. As sometimes happens when a closer enters in a nonsave situation, Chapman got a bit sloppy. His velocity was down—barely touching 100—and he gave up two runs in garbage time, but not enough for the Dodgers to come back.

The Cubs won, 8–4, and led three games to two, coming home to Wrigley Field for a potential clinching Game 6.

As was the case for the flight to Los Angeles, I couldn't be too choosy for the flight home. It left LAX at 5:30 p.m. That meant we would likely have to fight Friday LA rush-hour traffic to get there, so we left four hours before the flight, figuring to beat most traffic and have a couple hours to kill at the airport.

Unfortunately, I missed an exit and wound up having to take a circuitous route through half the LA metro area, or so it seemed. Including getting stuck in traffic at the airport itself on the rental-car shuttle bus, it took two and a half hours, leaving maybe 30 minutes at the gate area.

LA traffic. Can't imagine why people put up with it.

Back in Chicago, the anticipation of Game 6 was both exciting and a bit frightening, as the Cubs had been in this precise position before, 13 years earlier, coming back to Chicago one game short of the World Series, with Mark Prior and Kerry Wood scheduled to pitch. What could go wrong?

But these weren't those Cubs, and in fact, it was the opposition who had their best pitcher going, another round from Clayton Kershaw, who'd shut down the Cubs so well in Game 2.

It would be Kyle Hendricks who would shine in Game 5, though. Hendricks's outing was nothing short of beautiful. He allowed just two singles, and one other Dodger reached on an error by Javier Baez. All were erased on the base paths, two on double plays, the other on a pickoff. Hendricks has been among my favorites since even before he made the Cubs' big-league roster. He barely cracks 90 on the pitch-speed meters, but in this age of faster and faster fastballs, he's learned to get outs by changing speeds and locating. It's just incredible to see him strike out hitters on his changeup—a changeup they know is coming but they can't hit it anyway.

Meanwhile, the Cubs scored early again, in fact, getting the lead off Kershaw on the game's first three pitches, a double by Dexter Fowler and single by Kris Bryant. Bryant scored on a single by Ben Zobrist. Fowler made it 3–0 with an RBI single after a double by Addison Russell in the third. Willson Contreras blasted a solo homer in the fourth and Anthony Rizzo one in the fifth, Wrigley Field literally shaking from the sound of the crowd after both of those homers, and after that it was all Kyle, until he allowed a one-out single in the eighth.

Joe came to get him and bring Aroldis Chapman in the game. Hendricks departed to an ovation where you could feel the love all 42,386 in Wrigley Field had for this man, this year, this team.

Chapman took just three pitches to get out of the inning with a double play—and that got the Cubs over a significant hurdle. The "five outs to go" thing had been on Cubs' fans minds for 13 years. With just one pitch, Chapman blasted the Cubs and their fans' hearts through that wall.

After a 1-2-3 last of the eighth, a clean inning awaited Chapman in the ninth. He struck out pinch-hitter Kiké Hernandez. Two outs to go.

Carlos Ruiz, the second pinch-hitter of the inning, walked on a 3–2 pitch.

Dave Roberts sent up a third pinch-hitter, Yasiel Puig. I had barely finished writing his name on my scorecard when he bounced a ball to Russell.

Who threw to Baez.

Who threw to Rizzo.

And the Cubs were National League champions for the first time in 71 years.

Tears flowed, real tears, tears cleansing the hurt of 1969, 1984, 2003 . . . none of it mattered anymore. The Cubs finally, at last, had pushed aside all the pain, all the losing, all the rough times and brought joy to the North Side of Chicago.

Fans partied in the stands as the players merrily danced on Wrigley Field, bullpen catcher Chad Noble with a "W" flag draped across his body. Fans partied in the streets around Wrigley Field, happily, cheerfully, with few or no bad actors—only six arrests were reported, none for anything serious.

Some fans brought hundreds of pieces of chalk to write messages of love on the outside walls of Wrigley Field to the team that had brought them such happiness, writing the names of long-gone friends and relatives who had lived and died without ever seeing what we had seen that night. Police officers smiled and gave thumbs-up to this happy vandalism, which was washed away the next day.

From my earliest childhood as a Cubs fan, I watched the World Series on television, always with someone else's teams in it.

Now the Cubs, my Cubs, our Cubs, were going to the World Series to face the Cleveland Indians.

Epilogue:

What This All Means

Writing immediately after the Cubs won the World Series—yes, it actually happened. It was a dream of ours for decades or more but it's no longer a dream, it's reality—it's difficult to put into perspective on all of this, especially putting these thoughts into words the morning after on adrenaline and two hours' sleep.

The Cubs are World Series champions. It still all seems somewhat surreal.

And that's not just me—it's the response I get from nearly every one of my friends who I've spoken to since the great moment Wednesday night, November 2 in Cleveland (actually early morning November 3, Cleveland time). After all these years of cheering for bad teams that never came close, or good ones that had victory snatched away (sometimes in soul-crushing fashion), it is difficult to wrap my mind around the fact that it really did happen. In real life, the baseball heroes I've rooted for in blue pinstripes really were the last team standing, jumping around celebrating at Progressive Field with thousands of blue-clad fans also there to celebrate with them.

Those fans celebrated with those of us who couldn't make it, and beyond that, for those who have come and gone, living and dying without ever seeing what we witnessed that night.

It's those people I thought of on the morning after the win, many of whom I knew well from the bleachers at Wrigley Field where I've made my baseball home for nearly four decades. They should be here too, celebrating with us, but life doesn't always work the way we want it to. Some of those folks passed away way too young, others lived good long lives and never made it. I think of Carmella Hartigan, who you might have seen at Wrigley or on TV, a woman with white hair and a pink baseball cap who used to take two buses from her North Side home to the ballpark every day. A number of years ago a reporter asked if she thought the Cubs would ever win for her to see it. Her response, which I'll never forget: "How long do they think I can wait?" She was 98 years old at the time; sadly, she passed away in 2002 at age 101, never having seen a Cubs World Series win. Though she was alive in 1908, she wasn't living in the USA at the time, arriving later as one of many immigrants who came to this country in that long-ago time.

There are so many others that didn't make it who I remember that I don't want to start naming names or I'll leave someone out, but know I keep the Cubs memories of every one of you in my heart as I savor this victory.

I think of Ernie Banks and Ron Santo, Cubs Hall of Famers who not only played with distinction for the club for many years, but who were the team's biggest boosters and fans. It's tremendously sad that those men weren't here to enjoy this party with all of us. So we hold them in our hearts and minds and know that they're with us in spirit.

So, too, all the men who broadcast Cubs games since the dawn of television: Jack Brickhouse, Harry Caray, Steve Stone, Milo Hamilton, Lloyd Pettit, Chip Caray, and among others. It was said at times that Brickhouse, who broadcast over 5,000 Cubs games, saw more bad baseball than anyone. Hey! Hey! Jack, the team finally did it. He'd be over the moon, and so would Harry, who did more to promote and sell this team nationwide over WGN-TV than anyone. It might be, it could be, it is! Holy Cow!

For radio broadcasters Bert Wilson, Gene Elston, Jack Quinlan, Vince Lloyd, and Lou Boudreau, you too, are remembered, especially Vince and Lou, part of the soundtrack of my childhood. The Cubs won, gentlemen, and for all the bad years you broadcast games where there seemingly was no hope, now there is only triumph.

This win, too, is for all the Cubs players who put on the uniform and never accomplished this feat, some of whom got to the World Series and didn't win it, others who were utter failures, putting together 90-loss season after 90-loss seasons. For those Cubs, we celebrate with you today, from the bench players barely remembered to players like Billy Williams and Fergie Jenkins, or like Ernie and Ron Hall of Famers, who threw out ceremonial pitches at the World Series and are still here to enjoy this accomplishment. For Ryne Sandberg, too, another Cubs Hall of Famer who played for teams that came achingly short of the ultimate goal.

Theo Epstein is now likely headed, someday, to the Hall of Fame himself after ending the two longest droughts in baseball history, 86 years for his hometown Red Sox and now 108 years for the Cubs.

For many years I considered Red Sox fans sort of our "big brothers." They would get to the World Series from time to time after their last win in 1918 (over the Cubs)—in 1946, 1967, and 1986, only to lose each time in heartbreaking fashion. The Cubs in that time span never got there, so we looked up to them as the guys we wanted to emulate.

Since then, though, Red Sox fans have not been viewed quite so favorably as they won two more World Series and at times appeared to put on airs of superiority they hadn't shown before their drought was broken in 2004.

My hope for us is that we don't do that. This win has been so cathartic for every single Cubs fan, as all of us remember all the losing seasons of our lifetimes and all the near-misses in postseason play before 2016, that I hope each and every one of us keeps that in our hearts, understands how hard it is to win, and that we can stay humble as our team is on top of the baseball heap.

And at last, we bury forever all the talk of black cats, goats, and other "jinx" and "curse" nonsense, and forgive Steve Bartman.

Come back to the ballpark now, Steve, and enjoy the team we know you still love as much as the rest of us do.

It's simple. No "jinx" or "curse." The Cubs didn't win for 108 years because they just weren't good enough. In 2016, at last, they were.

Never forget where you were at 11:47 p.m. Central time on November 2, 2016, the day the Cubs won the World Series. Yes, you saw it, and yes, it really did happen.

Now let's do it again next year!

Acknowledgments

The first words of thanks from me have to go to the Chicago Cubs. Thank you, Cubs, for being the team I've dreamed of my whole life. I'd always wondered what it would feel like to be a fan of the team that won the World Series. And now I know. It's elation, it's joy, it's satisfaction that all the hours, days, months and years of passion for this sport and team at last ended in victory. Every moment, from failure to success, was worth it.

I can't say it enough: thank you, Cubs.

Thank you, Tom Ricketts, for never wavering in your quest to bring this title to all of us, and also for your personal kindnesses, and to Crane Kenney, who's also been kind and helpful to me throughout the nearly 20 years I've known him.

I could not have completed this project without the help and support of Niels Aaboe, Jason Katzman, and Ken Samelson at Skyhorse, men who believed in me to get this done under unbelievably tight time pressure while I was out rooting for the team and traveling halfway across the country to see the Cubs on part of the journey. I'm grateful to them and to all those on the production team at Skyhorse who were able to put this book together so quickly after the World Series ended.

Thanks to Pat Hughes for sharing his thoughts and feelings about this championship season in the foreword. Pat's an incredibly gracious man and I'm honored that he agreed to contribute to this project.

Thanks to Tyler Bleszinski and Markos Moulitsas (the latter, celebrating with me as he's a huge Cubs fan), who took a chance on me when starting up a fledgling group of blogs originally simply called "Sports Blogs," which became SB Nation, now part of Vox Media. They allowed me to take my passion for the Cubs and turn it into rewarding work, and I'm eternally grateful for their friendship. Thanks in particular to Jim Bankoff, Kevin Lockland, Lauren Fisher, Grant Brisbee, Sarah Kogod, Chris Thorman, and Justin Bopp at SB Nation/Vox for their assistance, guidance and support, and to my Bleed Cubbie Blue contributors Josh Timmers, Russ La Croix, Danny Rockett, Rob Huff, Tim Huwe, and Duane Pesice, who helped make 2016 a memorable season on the site.

Thanks to my friend Sue Skowronski, whose photos from Wrigley Field grace this book.

To my friend and colleague Rob Neyer, my eternal thanks to you for making me a better writer. I'm so glad you got to experience a game with me in the Wrigley bleachers during the Cubs' championship season.

None of this would have been possible without the years I spent in the Wrigley Field bleachers and the people I met there, first in right field, then moving to left when the bleachers were first rebuilt in 2006. If I try to mention every single one of you, I'm sure I'll leave someone out so just know that I think fondly of every one of you, everyone who's touched my life in the bleachers, thank all of you collectively for four decades' worth of fun, laughter, passion and sharing of a unique baseball experience. There's nothing like the Wrigley bleachers anywhere in sports, and I have made life-long friends from among people I never knew before I met them in the bleachers. Particular thanks to Mike Bojanowski, with whom I have shared literally thousands of games on bleacher benches at Wrigley; he's been a trusted friend not just at baseball games and answering any baseball historical question I needed answered (and always, every single time correctly), but through life. Thanks, too, to all the Wrigley Field game-day employees who went above and beyond the call to be gracious and helpful no matter what I asked.

Thanks to the following Cubs people who always had an answer for my questions: Julian Green, Peter Chase, Jason Carr, Kevin Saghy, and Alyson Cohen, as well as baseball historian Ed Hartig, always accessible and always helpful.

To my children: my daughter Rachel, not really a baseball fan but understanding of the love her dad has for the sport—thank you for your patience with my passion. And to my son Mark, a true Cubs fan like all the rest of us, and proud wearer of a Kyle Schwarber jersey, as he prepares to graduate from the same school Kyle attended, Indiana University.

To my dad, who is almost 95 years old and remembers the 1945 World Series and Cubs teams before that, though he's not as big a fan as I am: thank you for taking me to my first game at Wrigley Field, the beginning of a lifelong love for this team that culminated in this glorious season.

The last and most heartfelt thanks go to Miriam Romain, fellow Cubs fan and my life partner, who has given me more in every way than I can ever properly thank her for. We made it, Mir. The Cubs won.